CHEF GINO'S

TASTE TEST

CHALLENGE

Chef Gino's
TASTE TEST
CHALLENGE

100+ WINNING RECIPES THAT ANY KID CAN COOK

GINO CAMPAGNA

ILLUSTRATIONS BY MIKE LOWERY

RODALE KiDS

An Imprint of Rodale Books
400 South Tenth Street, Emmaus, PA 18098
Visit us online at www.rodalekids.com

Printed in China
Rodale Inc. makes every effort to use acid-free ∞, recycled paper ♲.

Illustrations by Mike Lowery
Photographs by Mitch Mandel, Matt Rainey, and Ryan Olszewski (all Rodale Images)

Book design by Christina Gaugler

Library of Congress Cataloging-in-Publication Data is on file with the publisher.

ISBN 978-1-62336-886-9   hardcover

Distributed to the trade by Macmillan

2 4 6 8 10 9 7 5 3 1

This book is for my wife, Laura,
and my children, Rocco and Ada.

But, of course, it's also for my mom, Pina.

And for my dad, Ettore, who, if they sell books
in heaven, would be so proud of his little Gino.

CONTENTS

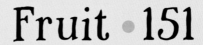

DEAR PARENTS,

My name is Gino Campagna. I come from Italy, Parma to be exact, the food capital of the world. Parmigiano-Reggiano comes from Parma, too, as does prosciutto di Parma and many other delicacies.

I was born in a house in a little square in the poorest neighborhood in town, but you didn't need to go any farther than that little square to find the most amazing food you'd ever tasted. I remember Cecé, a *pasticceria* with the most delicious pastries. Andrea, the pastry store owner's son, was my best friend, so it was not unusual for us to sneak into the back of the store to taste custard and whipped cream, trying not to be kicked out by the busy workers!

To the left of my house, there was a bakery, where every day I would go and buy fresh bread for my family—always the same order of typical Parma bread, two *ricce* and two *micche*, except for Saturday when I would also get a *miccone*, a larger loaf for Sunday. The baker's wife would give us kids free focaccia at the end of the day, as it would be a crime to try to sell 1-day-old focaccia to paying customers. The focaccia was soft and fluffy inside and crunchy and salty on the surface; in Parma it's called *torta salata* (salted cake).

For fruits and vegetables you'd go to Pino, the vegetable store owner who was helped by his cousin Berto. Pino would give away parsley for free just to get customers in, and I remember the summer fruits we would wait all year for—cherries, cantaloupes, and watermelons. Berto would cut a little pyramid-shaped slice of watermelon for

CIAO!

YOUNG GINO

you to taste before you bought it, so that you'd know it was delicious. He would never, never sell you produce he would not consider perfectly ripe.

To the right of the square, Ugolina (what a name!) would sell fresh milk and candies in her little store, the *latteria*. I remember buying licorice wheels and "cockroach"-shaped candies for 1 cent apiece.

Finally, next to my house's front door, a grocery store owned by Signora Rina, where we would buy everything else—fish for Friday dinners, meats for Sunday's bollito, the cheese (as Parmigiano-Reggiano is simply called in Parma), and then Parma's pride: cold cuts like salame di Felino, prosciutto, culatello, cicciolata, and mortadella. As a small child, I clearly remember imagining the world made of mortadella since I loved it so much: cars, houses, trees—all made of mortadella.

In my old neighborhood, the passing of seasons was always marked by distinctive flavors. In the summer there would be street festivals, and all the women would make their best ravioli and everybody would be eating them sitting around long tables set in the middle of the square, us children helping with the preparation and the serving of the food.

In the fall I would be sent to the local *osteria* to get some of the Oste's (the owner's) soup. I remember walking among wooden tables filled with men drinking Lambrusco wine and playing cards; my father, Ettore, would be talking about Sunday's football action. Everybody knew who I was.

The winter would always smell like street vendors selling roasted chestnuts and boiled chickpeas as you were walking home from school, and in the tiny apartment we lived in, you'd smell the orange rinds my grandmother Ada would leave over the stove to dry.

In the spring I would visit all the houses around the square with the local priest for the Easter's blessing. In every house a treasure of pastries, candies, and little snacks would await the altar boys. I would walk home with pockets full of treats for my brothers, Flavio and Andrea, and my sister, Barbara.

To be raised in Parma was for me a culinary luxury. I was also luckier than others because I was raised by the greatest cook in the world: my mom, la Pina. Growing up, my mom worked in the kitchen in the local nursery school a few blocks away from my square, a nursery school I attended as a child and where I worked once I got my teaching degree.

Cooking in a school in Italy is like cooking for the fanciest restaurant because no matter where you are in Italy, the food *has* to be great. At lunchtime in schools children sit at tables, with real plates and silverware, and they share their freshly made, delicious meals in a convivial atmosphere. My mom would go around the tables serving kids who would squeal in excitement as they were served delicious pasta or freshly made gnocchi, chicken alla cacciatora, and roasted vegetables.

My mom always considered herself a *cook* not a chef, with pride, with the understanding that the best food is always made at home. There's a story I always tell everywhere I go on my mission to raise American families' food IQs. I say that when Italians enter a restaurant, they know that, no matter how many Michelin stars the restaurant has received or how many cooking shows the chef has been hosting, the food will never be as good as their moms' food!

There's a lot of my hometown in this book, a lot of my mom, and a lot of the Mediterranean diet we didn't even know we were following—a diet that's not a diet as "let's follow some rules" but more like a lifestyle where well-balanced meals are enjoyed and appreciated for the variety of fresh and tasty ingredients used.

But this book also reflects another passion of mine: working with children. Once I got my early-education teaching degree, I started to work with children in schools, summer camps, and after-school centers. When, in the early '90s, I came to Los Angeles, a city I now call home, I immediately noticed the difference in American kids' food IQs from their European counterparts', and I made it my mission to teach American families how to both appreciate and prepare great, fresh, homemade food. The topic of children and food is hot these days with childhood obesity levels going up, but I decided early on to concentrate my efforts into celebrating great food instead of demonizing bad food.

Because of my background in education, I know very well that the lessons kids learn best are the ones taught through fun and play, and if you were to walk into one of the many classes I teach or live events I host, you'd feel like you walked into a party. I want children to see cooking as a fun activity, a bonding experience, an empowering adventure. I want to test their taste and challenge their comfort zone. I know very well that 99 percent of the kids I teach are *not* going to become professional chefs, but I know that all of them will, eventually, have to open a refrigerator trying to figure out what to eat.

And that's why I'm talking to you now before you step into the kitchen with your kids. The recipes in this book are simple, easy to follow, and tasty. They are also open-ended and easy to customize, modify, personalize—that's what makes cooking fun. The chapters will teach you basic concepts that once understood stay with you forever. Yes, once you learn about making crepes, you set yourself up for a lifetime of delicious French treats.

I've also included fun facts about food everywhere in the book; kids love a great story, and once they learn, for example, how many different colors of carrots there are, chances are they'd be more interested in tasting and cooking with carrots.

So should your children cook by themselves? Well, nobody knows your children like you do—so whatever you feel comfortable having them do, it's up to you. What I can tell you is that *supervision* is the wrong word—cooking is a team sport. Everybody can and should help. You'll notice that the ingredients listed in the recipes are "prepped"—chopped, sliced, and so forth. Depending on your children's age and skills, they could help you with that, too.

This book aims to encourage you to spend 20, 30 minutes together in the kitchen and more time sitting and enjoying the fruit of your labor. These are important moments in a child's life, where everybody in the family is together, without electronics (please!), talking, sharing the day's events and great food. Food that is made with love will be remembered with love—so put a little love in your cooking!

Buon appetito!

Chef Gino

Chef Gino's Tips for Cooking with Kids

What can kids do?
Preschoolers: mixing, pouring, kneading, spreading
Elementary school kids: reading and planning
the recipe, measuring
Preteens: pretty much everything!

Make sure you're comfortable with kids using knives,
and make sure children are supervised while cutting
and while close to heat.

Take the kids shopping with you if you can,
explore the aisles, and ask information about the food.
Even better: Find a local farmers' market
and go and have fun.

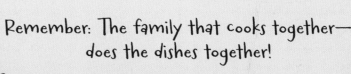

When buying ingredients, remember that:
Fresh is always best.
In season is even better.
Organic is great if you can.

Remember: The family that cooks together—
does the dishes together!

If they cook it, they will eat it.

CIAO, GUYS!

Welcome to my book.

You will soon realize that this is not a simple book of recipes; that would be—what's the word?—boring!

In this book, I really want to challenge *you* to test your taste. I want to challenge you to try different ingredients from the ones I suggest; I want you to come up with recipes based on the ones I wrote, but better!

Come on! Make your own version. Do you like spicy? Spice it up! You don't like an ingredient? Come up with a substitute that makes sense within the recipe—and, no, substituting chocolate for everything is *not* what I'm talking about. Otherwise you'd be eating chocolate—everything!

You have to be able to be creative, to have fun, to mess things up—shhh, don't tell your parents! They'll think you're just making a healthy meal.

Food is a *fun* thing to play with (Hey! No running in the kitchen!), but remember at the end of every recipe, you have to eat what you make! Sometimes you'll like it, sometimes you won't, but it's important to try.

I know you will soon find flavors you didn't expect to like, combinations you just can't get enough of; in no time you'll be making up recipes and inviting your friends over to test them.

Hey, did I say this is *my* book?!

Well, I was wrong!

This is *your* book of recipes!

Buon appetito!
Chef Gino

Chef Gino's KITCHEN RULES

1. Always read the recipe all the way through before you begin cooking.

2. Wash and dry your hands before touching any food or tools.

3. Assemble all of the ingredients you need and get out all of the equipment before you start cooking.

4. Make sure you check with a grown-up before you start using a knife or turning on the oven or stove top.

5. Pick up knives by the handle end only, and never point one at anyone else.

ONLY
PICK UP HERE

6. Use a stool if you need to be higher to chop vegetables or stir things on the stove top.

7. Clean up as you go: Throw away scraps and peelings, and place dirty dishes and utensils by the sink, ready to be washed when you are finished cooking.

8. Put cooked food on clean plates and not on a chopping board that was used for raw meat or any other food.

9. Before you leave the kitchen, clean up and make sure that the oven and the burners are all turned off.

10. Taste your recipe as you cook to make sure the flavor is right, and add what you like to make it your own creation.

NO FOOD HERE

MMM!

ON OFF

TOOLS

You can make most of the recipes in this book with a few simple kitchen tools; some of them are listed here.

PEELER

Use to peel potatoes, apples, or any fruit or vegetable with a skin that you want to remove. Can also use to slice veggies like zucchini and carrots very thin.

POTATO MASHER OR RICER

Use these to mash potatoes and other vegetables.

ROLLING PIN

Use to flatten dough for pizza, rolls, cookies, or crusts.

RUBBER SPATULA
Use to scrape the sides of mixing bowls.

PIZZA CUTTER
Use to cut pizza, pasta noodles, and dough to create fun shapes.

LETTUCE KNIFE
This knife is designed to cut lettuce without bruising or browning, and it makes a great first knife to practice your cutting skills.

WIRE WHISK
Use to whip eggs or cream or to add air to batter.

CUTTING BOARD
Use when you're chopping vegetable or fruit.

WOODEN SPOON
Use for stirring sauces, mixing hot or cold food.

MEASURING CUPS

Use to measure flour, sugar, and other ingredients for baking or cooking.

MEASURING SPOONS

Use to measure out spices and other wet and dry ingredients.

GRATER

Use to shred or grate cheese and other foods to scatter over your meal.

POT HOLDER OR GLOVE

Use these to protect your hands when handling hot pans on the stove and taking pans out of the oven.

SAUTÉ PAN

Use when you need to brown meat or sauté vegetables.

COLANDER/STRAINER

Use to drain the water from cooked pasta, or to wash fruit or vegetables.

MIXING BOWLS
Use small, medium, or large bowls for mixing ingredients.

SMALL SAUCEPAN
Use to heat up sauces or boil eggs.

LARGE POT
Use for soups or to boil water for pasta.

BAKING SHEET
Use this thin metal pan with low sides to bake cookies or other foods.

SOUPS

In this chapter, I'm challenging you to test your taste with something that can be made with virtually everything—soups! There's nothing better than a hot, steamy cup of soup to keep you warm in the autumn or the winter—hey, wait a minute, I live in Southern California, and it's always hot here! Even though we don't have a cold climate, I still enjoy soups because in the liquid you get all of the minerals and vitamins of the vegetables you've been using. So it's a super-efficient way to eat your veggies, and it's very nourishing, too.

GINESTRONE

AKA MINESTRONE

YAY! SOUP!

The Ginestrone is an easy recipe: All you have to do is put the ingredients in a pot half-filled with water and cook it! It reminds me of the old Stone Soup folktale, where everybody in the village added ingredients for the greatest soup ever. Feel free to mix and match vegetables here; be creative. I love veggies like celery and potato, but you could add broccoli florets and bell peppers, too, if you have those.

INGREDIENTS

1 small onion, peeled and diced

1 cup peeled and diced butternut squash

1 small potato, peeled and diced

½ cup green beans, trimmed and diced

1 carrot, peeled and diced

1 cup diced cauliflower

1 stalk celery, diced

1 zucchini, diced

1 cup peas

Salt and pepper, to taste

FACT:

Onion is Latin for "large pearl." Think about it: When peeled, it looks like a pearl!

DIRECTIONS

Put all the ingredients in a large soup pot half-filled with cold water. Cook over medium heat until the soup boils. Then simmer on low until the vegetables are soft and/or the water reduces by a third or half.

TIP: Have any Parmigiano-Reggiano cheese rinds in your fridge? Add a piece of the rind to the pot with all the vegetables. Remove it before serving, and you'll enjoy extra-cheesy flavor in your Ginestrone.

ALLIGATOR PEAR SOUP

AKA COLD AVOCADO SOUP

Did you know that alligator pear is another name for avocado?
Think about it: Doesn't it look like a pear with alligator skin?

INGREDIENTS

1 cucumber, peeled

2 avocados, peeled and chopped

2 tablespoons mint leaves

10–15 leaves parsley (or to taste)

Juice of 1 lime

1 cup milk or heavy cream

Salt and pepper, to taste

Sour cream or Greek yogurt
and chopped chives for garnish

DIRECTIONS

Put all of the ingredients except for the garnish in a blender and blend
until smooth. Add a dollop of sour cream or Greek yogurt, and scatter
some chives on top for decoration.

FACT:

You can ripen avocados by putting
them in a brown paper bag and
keeping them at room temperature.
Add an apple and a banana to the bag;
they will ripen faster, too.

3

MIGHTY MEAT BROTH
AKA BEEF AND CHICKEN BROTH

This recipe reminds me of my hometown of Parma and of my dad, Ettore. In Parma kitchens, it is not unusual to see really big soup pots filled with meats and vegetables in a hot, delicious broth. You can smell it the moment you walk through the doors of homes or restaurants. My dad wasn't much of an eater (I take after my mom)—but he insisted every Sunday was for his Mighty Broth, maybe with a little pasta in it. I will always remember how the steam from the soup would cloud his glasses as he never wanted to wait for the soup to get a little colder before eating it. Ciao papà!

INGREDIENTS

1 onion, unpeeled

2 stalks celery

2 carrots, unpeeled

1 chicken leg and thigh

1 small beef shank (approximately ½ pound)

Salt and pepper, to taste

DIRECTIONS

Put all of the ingredients in a large soup pot half-filled with cold water. Cook over low heat for at least 3 to 4 hours. Note: Keep the boiling to a minimum, and use a spoon to skim off the foam that forms on the top of the soup every 30 minutes.

Have an adult help you strain the soup before serving. Discard or compost the cooked vegetables. You could discard the boiled meat, but you could also eat the boiled meat and vegetables with the Salsa Anna (see page 59).

If you like pasta in your meat broth, add it here. Cook as per pasta instructions. Great for noodles and tortellini (see page 38).

SOUP'S ON!

WHOLE LOTTA SOUP

AKA VEGETABLE SOUP WITH POTATO AND FARRO

You know why I like this recipe? I like to say farro (farroh!). When you pronounce it, you can't help sounding Italian. Try it—with a little Italian attitude. Mamma mia!

INGREDIENTS

2 cups farro

2 tablespoons olive oil

1 small onion, peeled and chopped

2 carrots, peeled and chopped

2 stalks celery, chopped

1 potato, peeled and chopped

2 cups vegetable broth

1 cup cherry tomatoes

1 teaspoon dried oregano

Salt and pepper, to taste

DIRECTIONS

Put the farro in a bowl and cover with water for an hour. Drain and rinse the farro several times.

In a large soup pot, heat the oil over medium heat. Add the onion, carrots, celery, and potatoes and cook for 4 minutes. Add the broth, cover, and cook on low for 15 minutes.

Add the farro and tomatoes and cook covered for another 20 minutes. Add the oregano and salt and pepper.

VELLUTATA

(blended carrot and squash soup)

AKA CARROT SMOO* SOUP

(*smoo, as in short for "smooth")

Thanksgiving is the only time when Mrs. Chef Gino and my kids cook all the food. I love it, and I love Thanksgiving as it is my favorite American holiday. There's nothing wrong with a holiday that celebrates friends and family and great food! My contribution to the feast is this simple soup. I serve it in small glasses, and people just sip it like a drink—no spoons required.

INGREDIENTS

2–3 tablespoons olive oil

1 onion, peeled and chopped

1 clove garlic, peeled

2 large carrots, peeled and chopped

2 cups peeled and diced butternut squash

4 cups vegetable or chicken broth

Salt and pepper, to taste

Sour cream or Greek yogurt and chopped chives for garnish

FACT:

Carrots come in different colors—purple, white, red—even orange.

DIRECTIONS

Add the oil to a medium soup pot over medium heat. Add the onion, garlic, carrots, and squash. Cook for 5 to 8 minutes, or until tender. Add the broth and cook for 60 minutes over low heat. Add a sprinkle of the salt and pepper.

Once the soup has cooled off a little, have an adult help you put the soup in a blender and liquefy it.

Pour the soup into small drinking glasses or mugs. Add a dollop of sour cream or Greek yogurt, and scatter some chives on top as a garnish.

RIBOLLITA

AKA BEAN ME UP SOUP

Like every great traditional Italian recipe, ribollita was born out of the necessity to use up some 1- or 2-day-old bread. If you've got a hunk of hard, stale bread hanging out in your bread bin or in your freezer, then this is the perfect recipe to use it up!

INGREDIENTS

2–3 tablespoons olive oil

½ onion, peeled and diced

1 carrot, peeled and diced

1 stalk celery, diced

1 clove garlic, peeled and diced

1 cup peeled and diced red potatoes

1 cup shredded green cabbage

1 cup shredded kale (stems removed)

4 cups Mighty Meat Broth (see page 4) or cold water

Salt and pepper, to taste

1 can (15 ounces) cannellini beans, washed and drained

1 cup cherry tomatoes

4 slices 1- or 2-day-old rustic bread (or any type of loaf bread, really!)

DIRECTIONS

Heat the oil in a large soup pot over medium heat, and cook the onion, carrot, celery, and garlic for 5 minutes, or until soft. Add the potatoes, cabbage, and kale. Cook for a few minutes, and then add the broth or water. Add a sprinkle of the salt and pepper. Cook for at least 1 hour over low heat.

Add the beans and tomatoes. Stir and cook until the beans are almost a paste, adding more broth or water if the soup thickens too much. The ribollita should be a chunky soup, not watery.

Traditionally, you prepare the ribollita the day before you eat it; you can eat it right away, but it's really best the day after you make it. When the soup cools down, refrigerate and heat up on low heat in a large saucepan the next day. Toast the bread slightly. Place the slices in 4 soup plates, and pour the soup over the bread.

FACT:

Bread is the one food eaten by everybody around the world—every culture, race, and religion. It is also a universal symbol of peace, so don't be afraid to break bread with someone!

9

NUTS ABOUT SOUP

AKA ALMOND SOUP

A sweet hot soup? Sounds weird, right? But I love almonds in all their glorious forms. This soup has almonds ground into a flour and in the form of milk!

INGREDIENTS

1½ cups raw almonds

4 cups unsweetened almond milk

1 cup sugar

1 teaspoon vanilla extract

1 tablespoon cornstarch

1 tablespoon heavy cream

2 cups About Crunches (see page 13)

FACT:

Almonds are members of the—peach family!

DIRECTIONS

Preheat the oven to 350°F.

Place the almonds on a baking sheet. Toast in the oven for 20 minutes. Once the toasted almonds are cooled off, put them in a food processor and grind to the consistency of flour.

In a medium soup pot, gently boil the milk with the sugar and vanilla over medium heat.

Meanwhile, in a small bowl, stir the cornstarch and cream together. Add to the milk mixture along with the almond flour. Bring back to a boil for a minute or two. Serve with the croutons.

CROUTONS

VERY BERRY CHILLER
AKA STRAWBERRY SOUP

This recipe is so easy. Remember: The strawberries have to be sweet and ripe! The best way to get the strawberries you want is to buy them when they're in season in your area of the country. For most of us, that's summertime. It's always good to buy fruits and vegetables when they are in season as that's when they taste the best.

INGREDIENTS

- 2 cups strawberries, stems removed
- 2 cups milk
- 1 cup Greek yogurt
- Sugar, to taste (depends on how sweet your strawberries are)
- 3–4 leaves mint (or to taste)

FACT:

What are those little black dots on the outside of strawberries? They are seeds! Strawberries are the only fruit with seeds on the outside of their skin.

DIRECTIONS

Put all of the ingredients in a blender and process until smooth. Chill for a few hours or overnight. Enjoy cold.

NANNY AMABILIA'S SOUP

AKA RICE AND MILK SOUP

My kids' nanny Amabilia is more like a family member than an employee. She is just the greatest, but when she had her own children, she would come to work so tired I would insist that she take a nap and then wake her up in a few hours with breakfast. But her greatest contribution to this cookbook is her delicious yet simple recipe for a rice and milk soup. Whenever I try to do it for my kids, they always remind me that it's not as good as Amabilia's!

INGREDIENTS

4 cups whole milk

2 cups white rice

½ cup sugar

2 cinnamon sticks

1 tablespoon vanilla extract

FACT:

There are so many kinds of milk—low fat, no fat, goat milk, almond milk, rice milk, camel milk . . . That's right! People drink camel milk, too!

DIRECTIONS

Add all the ingredients to a large heavy-bottom pot and bring to a boil over medium heat. Once it reaches a boil, cover, set heat to low, and allow to simmer for 20 minutes, stirring occasionally until the rice is fully cooked. Remove the cinnamon sticks. Serve warm.

YAWN.

ABOUT CRUNCHES

AKA CROUTONS

What else can I say about these? I just love crunchy stuff!
Have an adult help you with the oven part of this recipe.

INGREDIENTS

4 slices bread (peasant or rustic bread is best)

3 tablespoons olive oil

Salt, to taste

DIRECTIONS

Preheat the oven to 350°F.

Using a cookie cutter, press shapes out of the bread. Brush
lightly with the oil. Place the bread shapes on a baking sheet and
sprinkle with the salt.

Place in the oven and cook for approximately 10 minutes, or until
crispy or golden.

SALADS

Salads! Yes, yes, salads! If you say "I don't like salad," then you haven't tried out enough combinations! What's not to like about salad? You can test your taste with so many possibilities that you'll definitely find something you love.

I was raised in Italy with the concept of salad being simply lettuce and tomato, but now I love big salads with fun ingredients like boiled eggs and beans— wait, I have to go and make myself a salad now. You do the same!

GREEN BOATS

AKA LEAFY SALAD

Hey, why eat a salad on a boring plate when you can just load up a big, crunchy, tasty leaf with all the good stuff? And this salad is fun because you can eat it with your hands!

INGREDIENTS

½ head romaine lettuce

1 small carrot, peeled and chopped

½ bell pepper, chopped

1 medium tomato, chopped

½ cup bean sprouts

3 tablespoons extra-virgin olive oil

1 tablespoon balsamic vinegar

Salt and pepper, to taste

DIRECTIONS

Wash the lettuce, making sure to wash the base and up every leaf. Remove 4 large outer leaves and set aside on a serving plate. Give the remaining lettuce a rough chop and add to a medium bowl. Add the carrot, bell pepper, tomato, and bean sprouts to the bowl with the chopped lettuce.

In a small bowl, combine the oil, vinegar, and salt and pepper and whisk with a fork until combined. Add to the chopped lettuce mixture and toss until everything is coated in dressing.

Carefully spoon the salad into the lettuce leaves and serve. Eat with your hands!

SUMMER IN GREECE

AKA GREEK SALAD

I love olives and feta cheese and the combination of olive oil and lemon, and this salad has all of those elements!

INGREDIENTS

- ½ cup chopped cucumber
- ½ cup chopped tomato
- ¼ cup chopped red onion
- ¼ cup sliced kalamata olives
- ½ cup crumbled feta cheese
- 1 tablespoon freshly squeezed lemon juice
- 3 tablespoons extra-virgin olive oil
- Salt and pepper, to taste

DIRECTIONS

In a large bowl, combine the cucumber, tomato, onion, olives, and cheese.

In a small bowl, combine the lemon juice, oil, and salt and pepper. Pour over the salad and mix until everything is coated in dressing.

FACT:

Olives come from—olive trees! On average, an olive tree can live from 300 to 600 years!

17

MOZZARELLA

BASIL   TOMATOES

ITALIAN FLAG SALAD

AKA CAPRESE SALAD

The caprese salad takes its name from the little Italian island where it was created: Capri. This is the ultimate Italian patriotic recipe as it has the colors of the Italian flag: red tomatoes, white mozzarella, and green basil.

INGREDIENTS

2 large tomatoes

1 large ball fresh mozzarella cheese

5–10 leaves basil, torn

1 tablespoon extra-virgin olive oil

1 teaspoon balsamic vinegar

Salt and pepper, to taste

TIP: Never cut basil with a knife or scissors! It will get dark pretty fast and won't look good. Always use your fingers to rip the basil into little pieces.

18

DIRECTIONS

Thinly slice the tomatoes and cheese. Begin arranging your salad: Place a tomato slice down on your plate as a starter, then place a slice of cheese down, and repeat until all the slices of tomato and cheese are used. Sprinkle with the basil. Drizzle with the oil and vinegar. Season with the salt and pepper.

BUFFALO MILK?

FACT: Mozzarella in Italy is mostly made with what we call Italian water. What's Italian water, you say? Buffalo milk!

BEAN SUPREME
AKA HIGH-PROTEIN BEAN SALAD

Beans, beans, and more beans! This is a great way to get your protein!

INGREDIENTS

½ can (7.5 ounces) cannellini beans, washed and drained

½ can (7.5 ounces) chickpeas, washed and drained

½ can (7.5 ounces) red beans, washed and drained

1 hard-boiled egg, peeled and chopped

1 bunch parsley, leaves chopped

½ red onion, peeled and chopped

Salt and pepper, to taste

4 tablespoons extra-virgin olive oil

Juice of ½ lemon

DIRECTIONS

In a large bowl, combine the beans, egg, parsley, and onion.

Prepare the dressing by mixing together in a small bowl the salt and pepper, oil, and lemon. Pour the dressing in the salad and mix well.

TUNA SALAD
AKA SKINNY TUNA

I love mayo, but sometimes you want something a little different. Try this tuna salad on bread or spread over celery sticks! For a fun presentation, arrange the tuna salad in the shape of a fish on the plate!

INGREDIENTS

- 2 medium tomatoes, chopped
- 1 can tuna, drained
- 1 avocado, peeled and chopped
- 5–6 stalks cilantro, leaves chopped (discard stalks)
- 6 spring onions, chopped
- Salt and pepper, to taste
- 4 tablespoons extra-virgin olive oil
- Juice of ½ lemon
- 2 tablespoons capers (optional)

DIRECTIONS

In a medium bowl, combine the tomatoes, tuna, avocado, cilantro, and onions. Add the salt and pepper, oil, lemon juice, and capers, if using. Mix together and enjoy!

SALAD OF THE GODS

AKA SHRIMP SALAD WITH GREEK YOGURT

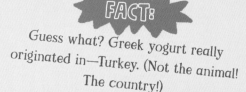

FACT:

Guess what? Greek yogurt really originated in—Turkey. (Not the animal! The country!)

Plain Greek yogurt is a creamy addition to a salad. Try to find one that is not too bitter; a mild flavor will give you volume without taking away from the flavor of the mayo.

INGREDIENTS

For the Salad

    4 cups cooked bay shrimp

    2 hard-boiled eggs, peeled and chopped

    1 avocado, peeled and diced

    2 stalks celery, chopped

    1 cup cooked corn

10–15 leaves parsley (or to taste)

For the Dressing

    ½ cup plain Greek yogurt

    ¼ cup mayo

    2 tablespoons freshly squeezed lemon juice

    2 tablespoons Dijon or yellow mustard

    5–6 large leaves parsley, chopped

        Salt and pepper, to taste

    4 stalks celery

DIRECTIONS

To make the salad: Combine the shrimp, eggs, avocado, chopped celery, corn, and parsley in a medium salad bowl.

To make the dressing: Combine the yogurt and mayo in a small bowl. Add the lemon juice, mustard, chopped parsley, and salt and pepper and mix well.

Coat the salad evenly with the dressing. Spread the salad on the 4 celery stalks.

FRUTA FRESCA

AKA MEXICAN-STYLE FRUIT SALAD

I'm loco for this recipe. In Los Angeles, where I live now, it's not uncommon to see street carts filled with chopped fresh fruit and ice to keep it cool. It's a great snack. I always ask for the grande (large), no pepino (that's the funny Spanish name for cucumber), no jicama (a type of Mexican turnip), and a little salt and lime but no chili powder—but you can make it any way you want!

INGREDIENTS

1 mango

1 orange

½ jicama

¼ pineapple (cut lengthwise)

¼ small watermelon (cut lengthwise)

¼ cantaloupe (cut lengthwise)

Juice of 3 limes

2 tablespoons salt

1 tablespoon chili powder

DIRECTIONS

Peel and pit the mango and cut into small strips about ½ inch in width. Peel and quarter the orange. Peel the jicama and cut into long strips. Remove the center rind and the skin from the pineapple and cut into strips about ½ inch in width. For the watermelon and cantaloupe, cut once down the middle and remove the rind from the outside. Then cut the insides into slices about ½ inch in width.

Add everything to a large bowl and give a quick mix. Add the lime juice and salt and mix one more time. Top with the chili powder and serve.

FACT:

Why is watermelon so refreshing? Because it's mostly made of water—almost 92 percent, to be exact!

23

EGGS ON THE RUN

AKA EGG SALAD SANDWICH ON WHEAT

I try to have breakfast at home with my family every day, but if I have to take my breakfast to go, then this is my favorite recipe. I like to prepare this the night before I need to get my breakfast on the go; it just tastes better if refrigerated overnight. By the way, whole wheat bread is more tasty than white here!

INGREDIENTS

- 2 stalks celery, minced
- 2 pinches salt
- 2 pinches pepper
- ½ cup mayo
- 2 tablespoons Greek yogurt
- 1 tablespoon yellow mustard
- 4 hard-boiled eggs, peeled and finely chopped
- 4 slices whole wheat bread, toasted

DIRECTIONS

In a medium bowl, combine the celery, salt, pepper, mayo, yogurt, and mustard. Mix well. Add the eggs and mix one more time.

Cover and allow to sit in the fridge overnight. Serve the next morning on whole wheat toast.

YUM

THE EARL OF SANDWICH

FACT: Too busy playing cards to sit down and eat, the Earl of Sandwich asked to have his meat between two slices of bread in the 1700s. He invented the sandwich!

PARMIGINO CRISPS

AKA PARMIGIANO WAFERS

These are small mounds of Parmigiano-Reggiano cheese baked into golden, crispy wafers, and they are so good! You can try to push the Parmigiano into cookie cutters—like you're making sand castles, but flat. Check out the illustration here to see what I mean!

INGREDIENTS

1 cup shredded Parmigiano-Reggiano cheese

DIRECTIONS

Preheat the oven to 350°F.

Place little mounds of the cheese on a baking sheet an inch apart. Place in the oven and let cook for just a few minutes until golden brown and rigid around the edges. You can also cook these using a nonstick skillet on the stove top over medium heat.

FACT: Parmigiano-Reggiano cheese takes its name from the two bordering cities where it's made: Parma (my hometown) and Reggio Emilia. But they forgot to mention Modena, another bordering city where it is also produced. Then it should have been called Parmigiano-Reggiano-Modenese— you're right: too long! How about: ParmiGINO?

MILAN

PARMA

ROME

LEAFY GREENS

These are the kinds of leafy greens I like. They taste good, and they have funny names or funny stories.

ARUGULA

Alternate names: Rocket, Italian cress, Mediterranean rocket, rugola, rugula, roquette, rucola

Characteristics: Coming from the Mediterranean, this green tastes peppery and is used a lot in Italy.

RADICCHIO

Alternate names: Chioggia, red chicory, red leaf chicory, red Italian chicory

Characteristics: Radicchio (what a name!) is a little bitter and has a beautiful red color, but when cooked, the red-purple color turns brown and what was once bitter becomes sweet.

ROMAINE

Alternate name: Cos lettuce

Characteristics: This is a large, leafy lettuce with a really crunchy, thick center. It's ideal for my favorite salad: the Caesar salad!

BUTTERHEAD LETTUCE

Alternate names: Butter lettuce, Boston lettuce, Bibb (limestone lettuce)

Characteristics: This is a type of head lettuce; the leaves of this lettuce are soft. And yes, like the name suggests, they taste as smooth as butter.

CRISPHEAD LETTUCE

Alternate name: Head lettuce or iceberg lettuce (the name iceberg was given to this lettuce in the 1920s when California lettuce growers began shipping lettuce in railcars filled with crushed ice)

Characteristics: This lettuce is tightly packed into a ball.

KALE

Alternate name: Leaf cabbage

Characteristics: Kale has green or purple leaves. Everybody loves kale these days!

SPINACH

Characteristics: This is an edible flowering plant that comes from Central and Western Asia. The spinach plant may grow up to 12 inches tall.

27

DRESSING MATRIX

Mix one ingredient from column 1, one ingredient from column 2, and as many ingredients from column 3 as you'd like.

1	**2**	**3**
extra-virgin olive oil	balsamic vinegar	mustard
vegetable oil	lemon juice	Worcestershire sauce
mayo	rice vinegar	crushed garlic
Greek yogurt	honey	paprika
	soy sauce	herbs de Provence
		dried oregano
		salt
		pepper
		wasabi

29

PASTA

Aaaahhh! Pasta! Or better, fresh pasta, or pasta all'uovo (egg noodles). There is nothing quite like it. I have hosted hundreds of classes around the world, but every single time I take out the pasta machine, I have to think of my mom, la Pina. My mom is a real rezdora; that's the dialect word they use in Parma to describe a person who can make a mean pasta!

How come something with only two ingredients, eggs and flour, can be so delicious and be made in so many different forms? All I know is that there's nothing like fresh pasta. Learn how to make it right, and you are set for a lifetime of delicious meals. You'll be the friend everybody wants to hang around with.

BASIC PASTA DOUGH

I start all of my pasta classes with the familiar, magical recipe of 1 cup flour with 1 egg. If you have 2 cups flour, then you'd use 2 eggs—even if you have 1 million cups flour, you'd use 1 million eggs! But sometimes 1 on 1 makes for a dry dough, so I recommend adding a little water or an extra egg yolk (like I've done below). That will make the dough a little more yellow—like they have in Italy!

INGREDIENTS

1 cup all-purpose flour

1 large egg plus 1 yolk

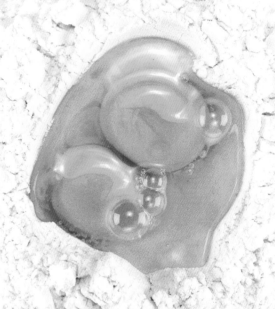

FACT:

Italian pasta makers from my area used to roll their fresh pasta on their dining tables using a very long rolling pin made of cherry wood. The best ones were able to roll the pasta in one single sheet covering the whole table!

Make a well.

Add eggs.

Mix with fork.

Knead dough with hands.

Form into ball and
wrap in plastic.

Flatten dough with pasta
machine or rolling pin.

DIRECTIONS

Make a well in the flour in a medium bowl or on a working surface. Mix in the egg and yolk with a fork, and then knead the dough with your hands. Wrap it in plastic and let rest in the refrigerator for 30 minutes.

Remove the plastic and use a pasta machine or a slightly floured rolling pin to flatten the dough into a thin sheet. The thinner the better—but make sure the dough doesn't break when it is flattened. Spread the sheet onto a floured surface. Now you can cut the pasta into any shapes you like!

To cook the pasta: In a large heavy-bottom pot, bring 4 to 5 cups of water and the salt to a boil over high heat. Have a grown-up help you carefully add the pasta to the boiling water. Cook for 3 to 4 minutes depending on the thickness of the pasta, or until cooked through. Carefully drain the pasta. Use the Pasta Sauce Matrix on page 44 to dress it, and enjoy!

FUN PASTA

BOW TIES AND MORE IN DIFFERENT COLORS

Why do I like homemade pasta so much? Because you can make it any shape you want, and if you add a little extra something, you can have colorful pasta! It's so fun to be creative with pasta.

INGREDIENTS

1 cup all-purpose flour

1 large egg plus 1 yolk

1 tablespoon tomato paste

OR

¼ cup spinach, boiled and chopped (you can use frozen spinach)

Pinch of salt

DIRECTIONS

Make a well in the flour in a medium bowl or on a working surface. Mix in the egg and yolk and tomato paste or spinach with a fork, and then knead the dough with your hands (you may need to add more flour if the mixture is too wet). Wrap it in plastic and let rest in the refrigerator for 30 minutes.

Remove the plastic and use a pasta machine or slightly floured rolling pin to flatten the dough into a thin sheet. The thinner the better—but make sure the dough doesn't break when it is flattened. Spread the sheet onto a floured surface.

Cut the dough into 3-inch rectangles. With your forefinger and your thumb, pinch the center of each rectangle, forming a bow-tie shape, and set aside.

In a large heavy-bottom pot, bring 4 to 5 cups of water and the salt to a boil over high heat. Have a grown-up help you carefully add the bow ties to the boiling water. Cook for 3 to 4 minutes, or until the pasta is cooked through. Carefully drain the pasta. Add to your favorite sauce or see the Pasta Sauce Matrix on page 44.

NOTE: You don't like BOW TIES? Well, use your imagination and create the kind of pasta you like!

PASTUFFED

RAVIOLI WITH RICOTTA AND SPINACH

This is my mom's best recipe. It's a classic dish the Parmesans (that's what they call people from Parma) eat all year round. But on the 23rd of June, when they celebrate San Joseph, they eat the ravioli very late at night, and then they wait for dawn so that after eating the ravioli, they can run through the dew in the grassy hills around the city: Crazy!

INGREDIENTS

- 1 cup frozen spinach
- 1 package (8 ounces) ricotta cheese
  or 1 cup fresh Ricotta (see page 43)
- ⅔ cup grated Parmigiano-Reggiano cheese
- 2 pinches of salt
- 1 recipe Basic Pasta Dough (see page 32)

DIRECTIONS

Add the spinach to a small saucepan, cover with water, and bring to a boil over high heat. Allow to boil for about a minute until completely thawed and warm. Strain and squeeze the spinach to remove excess water. Once the spinach is drained, give it a rough chop and add to a medium bowl with the ricotta, Parmigiano-Reggiano, and a pinch of the salt. Mix thoroughly. Cover and let sit in the fridge for at least 10 minutes.

As you wait, roll out the dough with a pasta machine or a slightly floured rolling pin into long, thin strips, and place on a floured surface.

Remove the ricotta mixture from the fridge, and spoon teaspoons of the mixture an inch apart down the length of the pasta dough strip until you run out of room. Place another strip on top. Firmly press the space between the fillings with your knuckles so that the filling is contained in the pasta. Then take a cookie cutter, pizza cutter, or knife and cut out each ravioli. Dip a fork in same flour and press it along the edges of the ravioli so that the edges are sealed. Place them on a floured surface and set aside.

In a large heavy-bottom pot, bring 4 to 5 cups of water and a pinch of the salt to a boil over high heat. Have a grown-up help you carefully add the ravioli to the boiling water. Cook for 3 to 4 minutes, or until the pasta floats to the top and is cooked through. Carefully drain the pasta. Add to your favorite sauce or see the Pasta Sauce Matrix on page 44. Serves 3 or 4.

Spoon the mixture an inch apart.

Firmly press the space between the fillings.

Take a cookie cutter and cut out each ravioli.

Dip a fork in some flour and press it along the edges of the ravioli so that the edges are sealed.

BELLY BUTTONS
AKA TORTELLINI

These are little round pasta shapes, and there is an Italian legend that says a chef in a Modena inn took inspiration from Venus's belly button shape to make the tortellini! I don't care what the inspiration was—they are just delicious.

INGREDIENTS

⅛ pound prosciutto, diced

⅛ pound mortadella, diced

¼ pound cooked pork, diced

½ cup grated Parmigiano-Reggiano cheese

1 yolk

Salt and pepper, to taste

1 recipe Basic Pasta Dough (see page 32)

Pinch of salt

FACT:

Italians call it mortadella, but in America it's known as—baloney! Why? Because the best mortadella comes from the city of Bologna in Italy. Baloney—it's just the Americanization of the word Bologna!

DIRECTIONS

In a food processor, combine the prosciutto, mortadella, pork, cheese, yolk, and salt and pepper. Blend until the mixture forms a thick paste. Spoon into a bowl and set aside.

Roll out the dough with a pasta machine or a slightly floured rolling pin into long, thin strips and place on a floured surface.

Make small squares of pasta 1 inch in size. Spoon a teaspoon of filling in the middle of every square, and follow the pictures on the opposite page for folding instructions.

In a large heavy-bottom pot, bring 4 to 5 cups of water and a pinch of salt to a boil over high heat. Have a grown-up help you carefully add the tortellini to the boiling water. Cook for 3 to 4 minutes, or until the pasta floats to the top and is cooked through. Carefully drain the pasta. Add to your favorite sauce or see the Pasta Sauce Matrix on page 44.

Move ingredients from the food processor into a bowl.

Spoon a teaspoon of the filling into the middle of each pasta square.

Fold the pasta square into a triangle shape.

Use your pointer finger to fold the triangle in half.

Use your other hand to press the top of the fold together.

Remove your finger!

39

VEGETAGNA

AKA VEGETABLE LASAGNA

Lasagna alla Bolognese is probably one of my favorite recipes. Although you can make the recipe below using the traditional Ragu Bolognese (meat sauce) (see page 55), this is my vegetarian version; it's just as good!

INGREDIENTS

Pinch of salt

5 sheets (recipes) spinach pasta dough (see page 34 for the dough directions), cut the same size as a bread loaf pan

1 tablespoon butter

2 cups chopped canned San Marzano tomatoes (or tomato sauce)

2 cups shredded mozzarella cheese

1 cup grated Parmigiano-Reggiano cheese

Salt and pepper, to taste

DIRECTIONS

Preheat the oven to 375°F.

In a large heavy-bottom pot, bring 4 to 5 cups of water and a pinch of salt to a boil over high heat. Have a grown-up help you carefully add the pasta to the boiling water. Cook for 3 minutes. Drain and dry on a tea towel.

When the pasta is cold, use the butter to grease a bread loaf pan and spread a bit of the tomato sauce and mozzarella on the bottom. Add a sheet of the lasagna and some of the tomatoes, mozzarella, Parmigiano-Reggiano, and salt and pepper. Keep layering until the last layer is tomatoes, mozzarella, and Parmigiano-Reggiano.

Cover the baking dish with foil and bake for 25 minutes. Remove the foil, lower the oven to 350°F, and bake for another 10 minutes.

Serves 3 or 4 people.

COCOA NOODLES

AKA CHOCOLATE PASTA IN CINNAMON SAUCE

Sweet pasta may sound like a strange idea. But this recipe uses unsweetened cocoa so you can also use this pasta for savory dishes—try it!

FACT:

The ancient Aztecs loved cocoa: For them, it was more precious than gold and money! For me, too!

INGREDIENTS

- ¾ cup all-purpose flour
- ¼ cup unsweetened cocoa powder
- 1 large egg plus 1 yolk
- 6 tablespoons unsalted butter
- ¼ cup white sugar
- ¼ cup dark brown sugar, packed
- 2 teaspoons cinnamon
- Pinch of salt

DIRECTIONS

Place the flour, cocoa powder, and a small amount of water in a bowl and whisk to combine. Make a well in the flour with your fingers. Mix in the egg and yolk with a fork, and then knead the dough with your hands. Wrap in plastic and put in the refrigerator for 30 minutes.

Use a pasta machine or slightly floured rolling pin to flatten the dough until it is quite thin. Once done, use the attachment of your pasta machine to cut tagliatelle, or fold the dough into thirds and have a grown-up help you slice lengthwise along the folded dough until you have many distinct noodles about ⅓ inch in width. Separate the noodles and place on a floured surface.

In a large skillet, melt the butter over low heat. Then add the sugars and cinnamon and combine until the sugar is dissolved. Remove from the heat.

In a large heavy-bottom pot, bring 4 to 5 cups of water and the salt to a boil over high heat. Have a grown-up help you carefully add the pasta to the boiling water. Cook for 3 to 4 minutes, or until the pasta is cooked through.

Strain and add to the butter-cinnamon sauce. Toss for 2 minutes over medium heat until the pasta is completely covered. Remove from the heat and the pasta is ready to serve.

PASTA DOODLE-DOO

AKA LEFTOVER SPAGHETTI FRITTATA

Why throw away yesterday's pasta when you can make it into a breakfast the next day, as well! I don't like to waste food in my house, so when I can reuse ingredients from the day before, I do.

INGREDIENTS

- 4 large eggs
- 1 teaspoon salt
- 1 teaspoon pepper
- 1 cup grated Parmigiano-Reggiano cheese
- 2 tablespoons olive oil

- ¼ cup chopped meat or vegetable of your choice, like pancetta, bacon, zucchini, peppers, or anything you like (optional)
- 3–4 cups already cooked leftover pasta given a rough chop (long pasta like spaghetti works best)

DIRECTIONS

Preheat the oven to 350°F.

In a medium bowl, beat the eggs, salt, pepper, and cheese until combined. Set aside.

In a medium ovenproof skillet, add the oil and cook the meat or vegetable, if using, over medium heat until crisp or cooked through. Add the pasta to the skillet and cook for a few more minutes.

Lower the heat and pour the egg mixture over the pasta mixture, stirring occasionally so that the egg coats the bottom of the skillet. Allow to cook for a few minutes, or until the bottom has finished cooking. Place in the oven for a few minutes and allow the top to set.

RICOTTA

Pay attention to this recipe because this is magic! Combine cream and milk with a little salt and lemon or vinegar—and you get cheese!

INGREDIENTS

4 cups milk

½ cup cream

Pinch of salt

2 tablespoons freshly squeezed lemon juice or vinegar

DIRECTIONS

In a heavy-bottom pot, bring the milk, cream, and salt to a boil over low heat. Once the mixture is boiling, add the lemon juice or vinegar and stir quickly. Wait for curds to form and remove from the heat.

Drain the mixture into a cheesecloth or a clean dish towel placed inside a strainer. When the ricotta is cold, close the cheesecloth with a knot and gently squeeze the excess liquid out. Open the cloth and put the ricotta in a small bowl and tightly pack it.

Put in the refrigerator for at least an hour. To serve, flip the bowl on a plate or cheese board and remove the bowl.

NOTE: When you bring the milk and cream to a boil, you can add a little honey, lemon zest, orange zest, or chopped herbs like rosemary and thyme. Time to test your taste!

43

PASTA SAUCE MATRIX

In Italy, you don't make the pasta swim in a sea of sauce like Americans seem to prefer; there's a great balance there.

This matrix will test your taste and allow you to make your own sauce. Remember the ingredients can be mixed and used with or without tomato sauce.

Mix one ingredient from column 1, as many ingredients from column 2 as you'd like, one ingredient from column 3, as many as you'd like from column 4, one from column 5, and one or two from column 6.

1	2	3	4	5	6
vegetable oil	onion	ground beef	mushrooms	Parmigiano-Reggiano	basil
olive oil	celery	ground turkey	fresh tomatoes	pecorino	oregano
butter	carrots	pork sausage	bell peppers	ricotta	parsley
	shallots	shrimp	zucchini	heavy cream	red-pepper flakes
	scallions	tuna canned/fresh	peas	mozzarella	
	spring onions	salmon	olives		
	garlic		spinach		

PASTA SHAPES

There are hundreds of kinds of pasta! Too many to list, but here's a bunch I like not only because they are YUMMY, but also because they have funny names and shapes! What's your favorite?

BOW TIES
Butterflies

CAPELLINI
Angel Hair

CONCHIGLIE
Shells

ORECCHIETTE
Little Ears

LINGUINE
Little Tongues

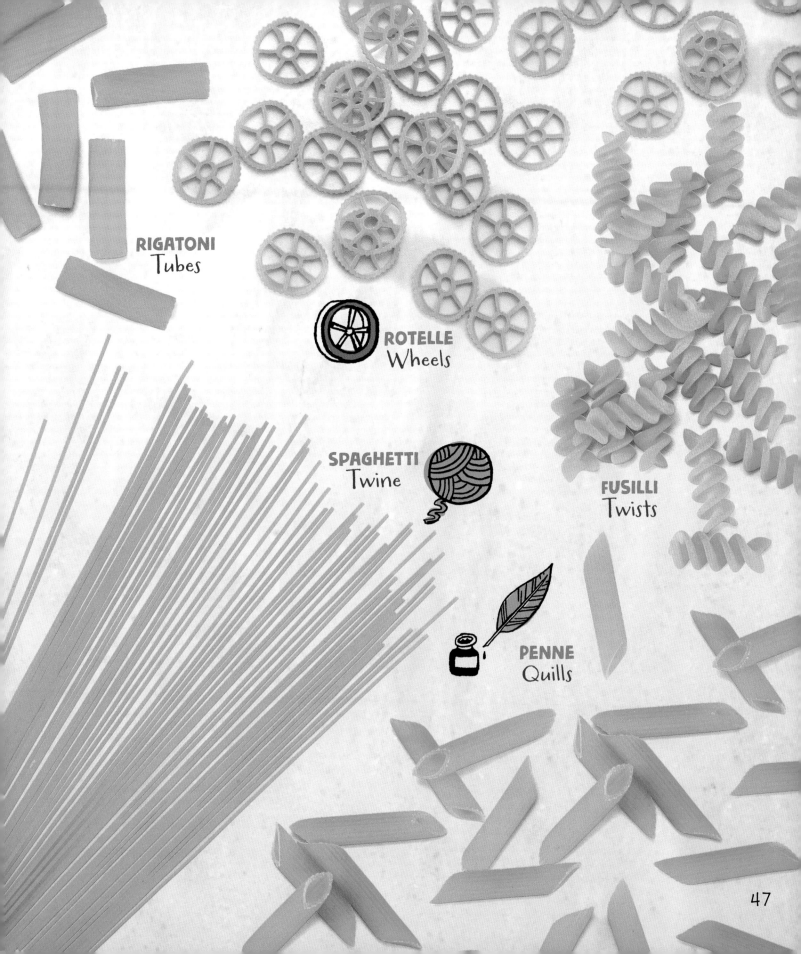

RIGATONI
Tubes

ROTELLE
Wheels

SPAGHETTI
Twine

FUSILLI
Twists

PENNE
Quills

47

STUFFED VEGETABLES

There are so many vegetables and so many ways to cook them: It's crazy! In this chapter, I challenge your taste with the concept of stuffed vegetables! Think of yummy vegetables stuffed with cheese or meat or even vegetables stuffed with—vegetables! The real challenge would be to stuff a vegetable and then stuff that vegetable in another vegetable, and so forth! That would be crazy. If you figure out how to do it—let me know!

ZUCCHINI BOATS

AKA ZUCCHINI STUFFED WITH MEAT

Another of my mom's favorite recipes, she would do it with leftover meat. Beware! You want to make sure the filling is cooked thoroughly—but you don't want to dry out the meat too much. That's something my mom would do sometimes—sorry, Mom, I never told you!

FACT:

When Christopher Columbus (in Italian, Cristoforo Colombo) brought pumpkins to Europe, Italian farmers were able to create the zucchini from them! Then later in the 1920s, Italian immigrants brought the zucchini to America! Hey, this veggie has traveled a lot.

INGREDIENTS

2 zucchini

1 tablespoon olive oil

½ onion, peeled and chopped

½ pound ground beef

Salt and pepper, to taste

2 tablespoons bread crumbs

2 tablespoons grated Parmigiano-Reggiano cheese

DIRECTIONS

Preheat the oven to 350°F.

Cut the zucchini lengthwise. With a spoon, scoop out some of the interior of the zucchini, making 4 zucchini "boats" (see the picture). Save the zucchini flesh for the next step.

Heat the oil in a large skillet over medium heat. Add the onion and zucchini flesh scooped from the zucchini. Cook for 3 minutes, or until the onion is brown. Let it cool and then mix with the ground beef. Sprinkle with the salt and pepper.

Divide the mix into 4 parts. Fill the 4 zucchini halves with the mix, sprinkle with the bread crumbs and cheese, and bake in a baking dish for 30 minutes, or until the cheese is brown on top.

MUSHBOOM!

AKA MUSHROOMS STUFFED WITH BREAD CRUMBS

I know, I know, kids in America don't always love mushrooms—but kids in Italy have grown up with them and love mushrooms, and I bet if you give them a try, you'll like them, too! In my early twenties, I used to work as a camp counselor in this mountain resort, and we often would go out (with a mushroom expert from the area) to pick mushrooms together. Remember: Don't pick mushrooms outside without the supervision of an expert—some are poisonous!

INGREDIENTS

12 champignon (button) mushrooms

2 tablespoons olive oil

1 clove garlic, peeled

½ cup bread crumbs

½ cup grated Parmigiano-Reggiano cheese

½ cup vegetable or meat broth

½ cup shredded mozzarella cheese

Salt and pepper, to taste

1 tablespoon chopped parsley

DIRECTIONS

Preheat the oven to 350°F.

Clean the mushrooms with a paper towel, separate the stems from the tops, and slice the stems.

Heat the oil in a medium skillet over medium heat. Cook the garlic until browned (so that the oil tastes like garlic) and then discard it. Add the mushroom stems and sauté until brown.

Put the mushroom stems, bread crumbs, and Parmigiano-Reggiano in a blender Add the broth a little bit at a time while blending until you create a dense paste (like the filling for ravioli)

Fill the mushroom tops with the mixture and top with the mozzarella. Bake on a baking sheet for 15 minutes, or until the tops are browned. Sprinkle with the salt, pepper, and parsley.

TOMATO BOOM BOOM

AKA BAKED TOMATOES STUFFED WITH RICE

The combination of tomatoes and rice is so great! Here you don't only have the tomato mixed with the rice, you also have a juicy tomato holding it all together. Double tomato, please!

INGREDIENTS

4 medium tomatoes

Salt, to taste

2 tablespoons olive oil

1 clove garlic, peeled

1 cup tomato sauce

8–10 leaves basil, torn

4 cups cooked rice

4 ½-inch cubes cheese (you could use mozzarella or Cheddar)

Pepper, to taste

DIRECTIONS

Preheat the oven to 350ºF.

Cut off the top part of the tomatoes (where the stem is) and empty them. Discard the flesh of the tomatoes. Sprinkle the inside of the tomatoes with the salt (just a pinch of salt per tomato) and turn them upside down.

Heat the oil in a medium skillet over medium heat. Cook the garlic until browned (so that the oil tastes like garlic) and then discard it. Add the tomato sauce and cook for 2 to 3 minutes. Add the basil.

Let the tomato sauce cool and add the rice, mixing well. Fill the tomatoes halfway with the rice, add 1 cube of the cheese per tomato, and fill the tomatoes the rest of the way with the rice.

Put the tomatoes in an oiled baking dish in the oven for 25 minutes. You can finish the dish by putting it in the broiler on high for 4 minutes. Sprinkle with the salt and pepper.

FACT:

Can you believe that tomatoes (technically a fruit) were once considered poisonous and were only used as decorations? What a waste!

TUNATOES

AKA COLD STUFFED TOMATOES WITH TUNA FILLING

Another stuffed tomato recipe: This one makes me think of summer, as my mom would prepare them when it was too hot to use a stove to cook!

INGREDIENTS

4 medium tomatoes

Salt, to taste

4 hard-boiled eggs, peeled

1 large can (12 ounces) tuna, drained

4 tablespoons capers

4 tablespoons sliced black olives

1 cup mayo

1 bunch parsley, stems discarded

Pepper, to taste

DIRECTIONS

Cut off the top part of the tomatoes (where the stem is). Spoon out the inside of the tomatoes and discard. Sprinkle the inside of the tomatoes with salt (just a pinch of salt per tomato) and turn them upside down.

In a blender, combine the eggs, tuna, capers, olives, mayo, and parsley. Put the blender on pulse and roughly chop the mixture.

Spoon the mixture evenly into the 4 tomatoes, sprinkle with the pepper, and refrigerate for 1 hour at least before serving.

BELL PEPPER COUS

AKA BELL PEPPERS STUFFED WITH COUSCOUS

Couscous is so easy to prepare and fast. If you need grains for your dish, then you can make a tasty couscous in about 5 minutes!

INGREDIENTS

1 cup couscous

1 cup warm vegetable broth

2 bell peppers, cut lengthwise

1 cup chopped tomatoes

½ cup chopped walnuts

½ cup dried cranberries

½ cup chopped black olives

¼ cup capers

8–10 leaves basil, torn

Olive oil

Salt and pepper, to taste

DIRECTIONS

Preheat the oven to 350°F.

In a large bowl, combine the couscous with the broth.

Seed the peppers and place side by side in an oiled baking dish.

In another large bowl, mix the couscous with the tomatoes, walnuts, cranberries, olives, capers, and basil.

Scoop the mixture evenly into the 4 pepper halves. Season with the salt and pepper. Sprinkle with the oil on top. Bake for 30 minutes, adding 1 cup of water to the baking dish halfway through.

FACT:

Despite me calling couscous a grain above, this food is not actually a grain! They are little balls made of semolina flour and water so technically, it's a pasta.

54

SQUASHETTI

AKA SPAGHETTI SQUASH BOLOGNESE

(as in spaghetti made of squash)

Note: If you're Italian, please don't read this paragraph as it will sound like madness to you! Guys, I think spaghetti squash is just as good as real spaghetti! I use the squash as a substitute for pasta all the time. You guys can do it, too. That means you can have larger portions since you won't feel as full because squash is not as heavy as pasta!

INGREDIENTS

½ spaghetti squash, cut lengthwise

2 tablespoons olive oil

½ onion, peeled and chopped

1 stalk celery, chopped

1 carrot, peeled and chopped

½ pound ground beef

1 can tomato sauce

Salt and pepper, to taste

¼ cup shredded Parmigiano-Reggiano cheese

DIRECTIONS

Preheat the oven to 375°F.

Take the seeds out of the squash, brush the external surface of the squash with olive oil, and place on a baking sheet skin part down. Cook in the oven for 25 minutes.

In the meantime, heat the oil in a medium skillet over medium heat. Add the onion, celery, and carrot. Cook until tender. Add the ground beef, using a spoon to separate the meat. When the beef is cooked through, add the tomato sauce and salt and pepper. Reduce the heat to low and cook for at least 15 minutes (it's a Bolognese sauce—the longer the better!).

Take the squash out of the oven and, with the help of a grown-up, when the squash is cool, scrape out the flesh of the squash with a spoon. The flesh should be of a spaghetti-like quality.

Add the "spaghetti" to the sauce while on low heat and mix. Serve with the cheese.

NOTE: If you want, you can keep the "shell" of the squash as a serving dish, pouring the Squashetti in it before serving.

CUCUMBER LOGS

AKA STUFFED CUCUMBERS

Got to be honest, cucumbers are not my favorite thing, but when you stuff them full of the ingredients below, they are so good!

INGREDIENTS

1 long cucumber

½ cup cream cheese or (even better) mascarpone, at room temperature

¼ cup chopped parsley

¼ cup chopped walnuts

¼ cup dried cranberries

1 tablespoon extra-virgin olive oil

Salt and pepper, to taste

FACT:

Cucumbers are full of history! It was the ancient Egyptians' favorite vegetable, and ancient Greeks and Romans thought it made you smarter—so I better start eating some cucumbers!

DIRECTIONS

Peel the cucumber with a peeler and cut into 2-inch logs.

Scoop most of the cucumber flesh out but leave the sides and the bottom, creating a little "cucumber bowl."

Mix the remaining ingredients in a large bowl. Use a pastry bag to fill the bowls with the mixture.

56

ADA'S APPLES

AKA STUFFED BAKED APPLES

Ada was my grandmother's name, and she loved baked apples. My grandmother basically lived with us and would help my mom with four kids running around the house. She used to love to make this recipe. She would simply bake the apples with a sprinkle of granulated sugar on top; the apples were so sweet back when I was growing up that they didn't need much else. I expanded a little on her basic recipe, but it still makes me think about her every time I prepare it.

INGREDIENTS

4 apples

4 tablespoons chopped walnuts

4 tablespoons chopped pistachios

4 tablespoons crumbled amaretti cookies

2 tablespoons raisins

2 tablespoons honey

1 tablespoon sugar

FACT:

Red Delicious, Gala, Fuji, Granny Smith, Honeycrisp, McIntosh—there are hundreds of types of apples; I could go on forever!

DIRECTIONS

Preheat the oven to 375°F.

Wash the apples. Core them, being careful not to take out the bottom part (see the picture).

Mix the nuts, cookies, raisins, and honey in a large bowl.

Place the apples in a baking dish. Fill them with the mix and sprinkle evenly with the sugar on top. Bake for 30 minutes, or until the tops are browned.

RING THE BREAKFAST BELL

AKA BELL PEPPER RINGS WITH EGGS INSIDE

This recipe is fun because it looks cool but also because the ring of bell peppers add a little more texture and flavor to the usual sunny-side-up eggs!

INGREDIENTS

1 bell pepper

2 tablespoons butter

4 eggs

Salt and pepper, to taste

DIRECTIONS

Slice the bell pepper to form 4 rings ¼ inch thick (see the picture). Discard the white seeded center.

Melt the butter in a large skillet. Place the pepper rings in the skillet and crack 1 egg carefully inside every one. Cook on medium heat until firm, or approximately 4 minutes. Flip the rings carefully and cook the other side for a couple of minutes. Sprinkle with the salt and pepper.

SALSA ANNA

AKA GREEN PARSLEY SAUCE

My Aunt Anna is also a great cook, and I remember many, many lunches and dinners at her house with my cousin Maura and my uncle Sergio. This is the sauce she'd prepare to go with the bollito mixed meat used to make broth (see my Mighty Meat Broth recipe on page 4). I never liked bollito very much, but I loved her green sauce, so I would have a little meat and a lot of sauce!

INGREDIENTS

- 2 tablespoons butter (you could also use olive oil)
- 1 cup finely chopped parsley
- 2 tablespoons tomato paste
- 1 tablespoon white wine vinegar
- 2 hard-boiled yolks (boil the eggs and discard the whites)
- Salt, to taste

DIRECTIONS

Melt the butter in a small skillet or sauce-pan over medium heat. Add the parsley, tomato paste, and vinegar and cook for 5 minutes. Add the yolks (some people like to add 1 anchovy) and cook for another 5 minutes. Add the salt. Serve hot or cold.

FACT:

My mom and my aunt love Italian parsley. They put it almost everywhere. They say someone who knows everything about everybody is like—parsley!

Favorite Global
RICES and GRAINS

These are the grains I like because they take me around the world!

ARBORIO
for risotto, from Italy

STICKY RICE
for sushi, from Japan

BARLEY
dates back to the Stone Age

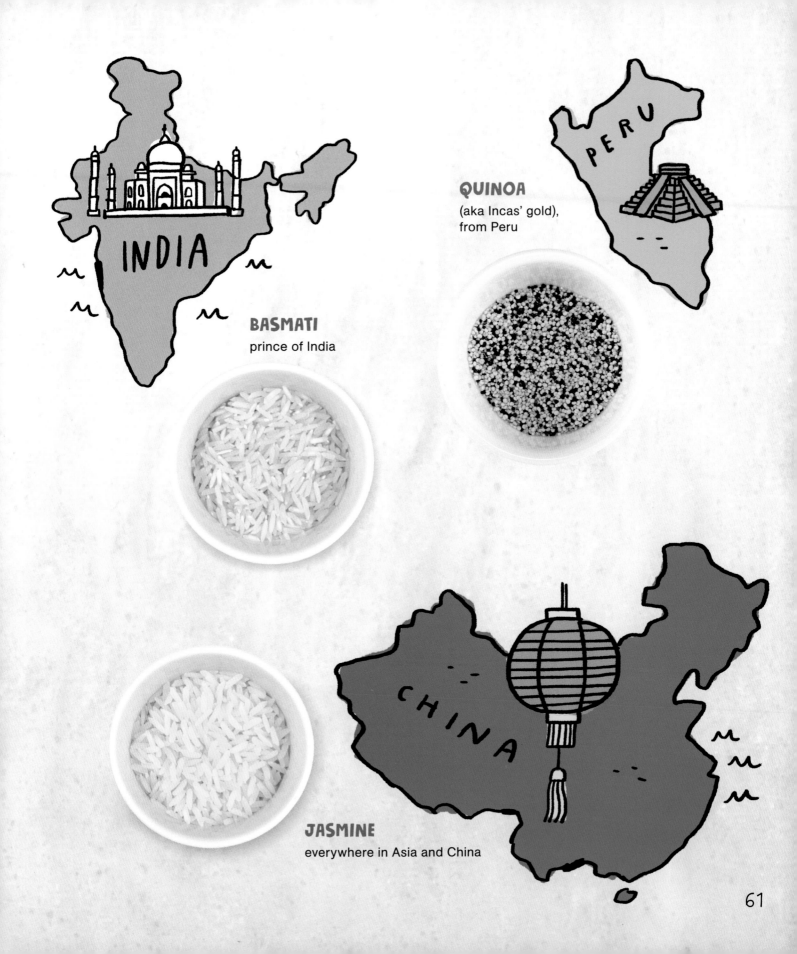

INDIA

BASMATI

prince of India

QUINOA
(aka Incas' gold),
from Peru

PERU

JASMINE

everywhere in Asia and China

CHINA

61

LAYERS

The concept of layering is perfect for challenging your taste. There's a dessert in Italy called millefoglie; it translates as "thousand leaves"— stacked together. A thousand layers—can you imagine what that would look like? A tower of flavor!

EGGPLENTY

AKA EGGPLANT PARMIGIANA

I wish I could say the name parmigiana comes from my hometown of Parma, but the truth is that it comes from the Sicilian dialect and means "layers." It makes sense since the most famous parmigiana is the eggplant one. In Sicily, you were not considered a true chef back in the day if you didn't have at least 40 different eggplant recipes inside your head.

INGREDIENTS

1 large eggplant, peeled and sliced (¼-inch thickness)

1 tablespoon butter

4 cups chopped canned San Marzano tomatoes

4 cups shredded mozzarella cheese

1 cup grated Parmigiano-Reggiano cheese

8–10 leaves basil, torn

Salt and pepper, to taste

DIRECTIONS

Preheat the oven to 375°F.

Place the eggplant on a baking sheet and bake until tender (approximately 20 minutes).

Oil a baking dish with the butter and spread a bit of the tomatoes and mozzarella on the bottom. Add a layer of the eggplant, tomatoes, mozzarella, Parmigiano-Reggiano, basil, and salt and pepper. Keep layering until the last layer is tomatoes, mozzarella, and Parmigiano-Reggiano. Bake for 30 minutes, or until browned on top.

FACT:

Eggplants come from India where they are considered the king of all vegetables (even though technically they are a fruit). In Italian, they are called melanzane, which translates as "insane apples" because when they were first introduced in Europe, people thought that if you ate melanzane, you'd go crazy! Crazy for eggplant, I'd say!

66

RAINBOW TOWER

AKA SALAD IN A JAR

No better recipe than this one to test your taste; there's no right way or wrong way to do this! You do it your way! If you do the layers carefully, it looks so pretty in a jar.

INGREDIENTS

- 1 cup peas
- 1 cup corn
- 1 cup chopped tomatoes
- 1 cup chopped red bell peppers
- 1 cup chopped celery
- 1 cup shredded carrots
- 2 teaspoons salt
- 1 tablespoon balsamic vinegar
- 4 tablespoons extra-virgin olive oil

DIRECTIONS

Boil the peas and the corn separately in medium saucepans filled with 2 cups of water over medium heat for a few minutes until cooked. Let them cool off in ice water and drain.

Take 4 mason jars and start layering the vegetables one at a time—in whatever order you like.

In a small bowl, prepare the dressing by dissolving the salt in the vinegar. Add the oil and mix well. Sprinkle evenly in the 4 jars. Close the jar, shake the jar to mix thoroughly, open the jar, and enjoy!

NOTE: If you're going to a picnic, close the jars and keep them in a cooler till ready to eat. Keep the dressing in a separate container and add to the salad jar when you're ready to eat.

VEGGIE SPIRAL

AKA VEGETABLE AND CHEESE CASSEROLE

This recipe has the prettiest colors, and the flavors are pretty good, too!

INGREDIENTS

- 1 medium potato, peeled
- 4 tablespoons olive oil
- 2 large green zucchini, thinly sliced widthwise
- 2 large yellow zucchini, thinly sliced widthwise
- 2 red bell peppers, seeded and thinly sliced widthwise

- 2 large tomatoes, sliced
- 2 cups shredded mozzarella cheese
- ½ cup grated Parmigiano-Reggiano cheese
- Salt and pepper, to taste

DIRECTIONS

Preheat the oven to 350°F.

Boil the potato in a medium pot filled with 2 cups of water over high heat until a fork can be easily inserted in it. Drain and cool the potato. Thinly slice it widthwise.

Brush the oil on a baking sheet, place the zucchini and bell peppers on it (you may need 2 baking sheets), and bake for 12 minutes.

When the vegetables are cooked and have cooled, layer them in a spiral pattern in an oiled baking dish: Spiral the potato slices, one-quarter of the tomato slices, and then sprinkle one-quarter of the mozzarella, and one-quarter of the Parmigiano-Reggiano over them. Add the salt and pepper, and continue spiraling the vegetables in the same fashion. Increase the oven heat to 375°F and bake for 25 minutes, or until browned on top.

TOMATOLIVE

AKA FRESH TOMATO AND OLIVE PATE STACK

I love olives, and I love olive pate (just put the olives in a blender with some oil). This is a great little snack, or it looks lovely on an antipasti (appetizers) platter.

INGREDIENTS

- 1 cup pitted black olives
- 1 clove garlic, peeled
- ¼ cup grated Parmigiano-Reggiano cheese
- 2 leaves basil
- 1 teaspoon grated lemon peel
- ¼ cup extra-virgin olive oil
- Salt and pepper, to taste
- 4 tomatoes, sliced widthwise

FACT:
There are so many kinds of olives! Some are best to eat, and some are best to squeeze and make—olive oil!

DIRECTIONS

In a blender, put the olives, garlic, cheese, basil, lemon peel, and oil. Add the salt and pepper and mix to a paste.

Take the slices of tomatoes and spread them evenly with the olive pate. Re-create the tomato stacks (see the picture).

ITALIAN FLAG GRATIN

AKA RED, WHITE, AND GREEN VEGGIE CASSEROLE

The secret of this recipe (or any recipe with vegetables!) is to pick the right vegetables. Make sure the zucchini are firm, not too big or they can taste a little woody. And make sure the tomatoes smell like tomatoes! That intoxicating, pungent smell reminds me of when I was a student in Italy and I used to pick tomatoes in the summer to make some money.

INGREDIENTS

3 potatoes, sliced ½ inch thick (with skin)

1 tablespoon olive oil

3 zucchini, thinly sliced

1 tablespoon butter

½ cup bread crumbs

3 large tomatoes, sliced

2 cups shredded mozzarella cheese

1 cup grated Parmigiano-Reggiano cheese

5 leaves basil, torn

Salt and pepper, to taste

½ cup milk

DIRECTIONS

Preheat the oven to 350°F.

Soak the potatoes in cold water for a few minutes. Boil 4 cups of water in a large pot over high heat and cook the potatoes for 3 to 4 minutes. Drain and let cool.

In a medium skillet over medium heat, add the oil and sauté the zucchini until soft. Set aside.

Take a baking dish (8-inch x 8-inch), grease it with half of the butter, and dust with half of the bread crumbs. Cover the bottom of the baking dish with a layer of the potatoes, loosely layer some of the zucchini and tomatoes, and sprinkle some of the mozzarella and Parmigiano-Reggiano, basil, and salt and pepper. Repeat until you run out of ingredients (hold back a few tablespoons of Parmigiano-Reggiano to sprinkle on top before baking). The top layer should be zucchini and tomatoes and mozzarella.

Pour the milk over the dish. Add the remaining Parmigiano-Reggiano and the rest of the bread crumbs and butter. Place in the oven for 40 minutes, or until browned on top.

ENGLISH TEA
sandwiches

I lived in England for a couple of years, and there's nothing like a Sunday tea in the countryside. Maybe it's raining outside, the hills are green, and the tea—hot, milky, and sweet! And then there are the little sandwiches! I love to sample! I'm in heaven!

INGREDIENTS

Bread slices, white and whole wheat

½ cup cream cheese

½ cup peeled and thinly sliced cucumber

4 slices ham

1 hard-boiled egg, thinly sliced

1 small tomato, thinly sliced

Olive Pate (see page 74), to taste

Carrot Crush (see page 116), to taste

Mustard, to taste

Mayo, to taste

Parsley leaves, torn, to taste

Salt and pepper, to taste

DIRECTIONS

Cut the bread with small cookie cutters, and do the same with the ingredients you can cut with the cookie cutters. Add or spread the rest of the ingredients.

Pretty much there's no wrong way, no right way—just make small double- and triple-decker sandwiches, layering the bread with your favorite ingredients.

OLIVE PATE

INGREDIENTS

1 cup pitted olives (green or black)

2 tablespoons olive oil

1 clove garlic, peeled

2 leaves basil

Salt, to taste (remember, olives are naturally salted—you may not need much salt)

DIRECTIONS

Put all the ingredients in a blender and make a paste.

BLUE SPREAD

This is not blue as in the color BLUE! It's blue because it uses blue cheese, which is a sharp creamy cheese. My favorite is Italian Gorgonzola Dolce.

INGREDIENTS

- ½ cup mascarpone cheese or cream cheese
- ½ cup creamy blue cheese
- 3 tablespoons walnuts

DIRECTIONS

Put all ingredients in a blender and mix till smooth like a spread.

BERRY GOOD TRIFLE
AKA LAYERS OF FRUIT, YOGURT, AND CRUNCHY TREATS

Trifle comes from the French word troufle, which means—"messy"! Messy is my favorite word in the kitchen! Do I have to challenge your taste with this one? I bet you find plenty of yummy things to go in it!

INGREDIENTS

1 cup crumbled cookies or angel cake

1 cup granola

1 cup chopped walnuts

1 cup blueberries

1 banana, sliced

1 cup chopped strawberries

1 cup plain or any flavor yogurt

1 cup whipped cream

Mint leaves for decoration

DIRECTIONS

There's really no right way, no wrong way to prepare this recipe. Just layer the ingredients the way you like in 4 mason jars or wide-bottom water glasses and enjoy!

NOTE: If you have some leftover mint leaves from the recipe, boil some water and let the leaves steep for a few minutes and enjoy a delicious mint tea! If you don't want to eat some mint, you may want to strain the tea before drinking it.

AVO TOSTADO

AKA AVOCADO TOAST WITH TOMATO AND EGG

This is a very popular recipe in hip restaurants across America—and why not? It's super tasty!

INGREDIENTS

4 slices whole wheat bread

2 ripe avocados

1 tablespoon lime juice

Salt and pepper, to taste

4 slices large tomato

2 tablespoons butter

4 eggs

DIRECTIONS

Toast the bread. Using a cookie cutter, cut a circle as large as you can in each slice.

Halve and pit the avocados. Spoon out the flesh into a small bowl and mash with a fork, ricer, or masher. Add the lime and salt and pepper and mix well. Spread on the toast circles. Top with the tomato slices.

Melt the butter in a large skillet over medium heat and fry the eggs to your preferred firmness. Sprinkle with the salt and pepper and place the eggs over the tomato slices.

PIZZA

Did somebody say pizza? Here's some great recipes to test your taste! Pizza is literally a canvas; once you prepare the dough, the toppings are up to you and your creativity. My all-time favorite pizza was one made in my hometown of Parma, which is not particularly well known for pizza like, let's say, Naples. It was in this little pizzeria in my neighborhood. The pizzaiolo (which means "the pizza maker") used to load the pie with the most delicious combination of vegetables: green beans, zucchini, spinach, rapini. Add a drizzle of extra-virgin olive oil on top before eating it— mamma mia!

BASIC PIZZA DOUGH

Here it is: Chef Gino's own pizza dough recipe. I don't know how many events and classes I have hosted using this basic recipe or how many lunches and dinners I have prepared for my family and friends! Remember, there's nothing wrong with pizza in moderation and as part of a balanced diet. That means: Don't eat pizza for breakfast, lunch, and dinner! Makes enough dough for 2 pizzas.

INGREDIENTS

- 1 package or 2¼ teaspoons active dry yeast
- 1 teaspoon sugar
- 1 cup warm water (between 100°F and 110°F so you don't kill, or chill, the yeast)
- 2 tablespoons olive oil
- 2–3 cups all-purpose or whole wheat flour
- 1 teaspoon salt

DIRECTIONS

Combine the yeast and sugar in a large bowl. Add the warm water and let sit for 5 minutes. Add the oil and stir well. Add the flour to the bowl in small amounts and stir well after each addition. Halfway through the process of adding the flour, add the salt. Add just enough flour so the dough is not sticking in clumps to your hands or the bowl.

Using your hands, knead the dough for 2 to 3 minutes on a lightly floured surface. The dough should be soft. Let the dough rest for 10 to 20 minutes before using.

Check out the next few recipes for ways to use this pizza dough!

FACT:

The most important thing when you bake pizza is the temperature—it has to be very hot. In fact, the first pizza ovens were made with lava rocks to sustain the high temperatures necessary to bake the perfect pizza!

Combine yeast and
sugar in a bowl.

Add the warm water and
let it sit for 5 minutes.

Add the flour in small
amounts. Add the salt.

Whisk together
into a dough.

Use your hands to
knead the dough.

Shape into a ball.

Place ball back in bowl and
cover with plastic wrap for
10–20 minutes.

Remove the dough and
stretch with your hands.

Place on a pizza plate
and stretch into a circle.

MAGIC MARGHERITA

AKA BASIC CHEESE PIZZA

This pizza takes its name from the queen of Italy at the time; her full name was Margherita Maria Teresa Giovanna di Savoia, but that name is way too long for a pizza. So they named it pizza Margherita. It also contains the colors of the Italian flag: red tomatoes, white mozzarella, and green basil. Buon appetito!

INGREDIENTS

- ½ recipe Basic Pizza Dough (see page 82)
- 2 tablespoons olive oil
- ⅔ cup San Marzano tomato sauce
- 1 cup shredded mozzarella cheese
- Salt and pepper, to taste
- 8–10 leaves basil, torn

DIRECTIONS

Preheat the oven to 400°F.

On a floured surface, fold and knead the dough with your hands until it is workable. Begin to spread out the dough using your knuckles. Once the pizza is about 7 to 8 inches in diameter and ½ inch thick, move to a 9-inch pan coated with the oil. Continue to spread out the dough with your hands until it covers the bottom of the pan.

Using a spoon, spread the tomato sauce on the dough, leaving 1 inch uncovered around the edge. Sprinkle the cheese over the pizza, making sure to cover the tomato sauce. Season with the salt and pepper and add the basil. Place in the oven carefully (have an adult help you with this) and let cook for 20 minutes, or until the crust is golden brown. Serve warm.

IN THE (CAL) ZONE

AKA CALZONE WITH VEGETABLES AND SAUSAGE

A calzone is like a more portable pizza. But beware, the filling stays hot for a while! If you make a small calzone and you fry it (again, be careful; deep-frying should be done with adult supervision at all times), you will have a panzerotto: a classic Italian street food.

INGREDIENTS

½ recipe Basic Pizza Dough (see page 82)

2 tablespoons olive oil

½ cup San Marzano tomato sauce

½ cup shredded mozzarella cheese

1 cooked Italian sausage, casing removed and crumbled

1 cup cooked vegetables of your choice

DIRECTIONS

Preheat the oven to 400°F.

Follow the instructions on page 84 to prepare the dough in the pan.

Once this is done, spread the tomato sauce on the dough, leaving 2 inches around the edge uncovered. Add the cheese, sausage, and vegetables to the center and fold over the dough, pressing down with your knuckles to seal. Place in the oven carefully (have an adult help you with this) and let cook for 20 minutes, or until the crust is golden brown. Serve warm (but remember, be careful because the insides are hot).

CRAZY CRACKERS

AKA CRACKERS AND GRISSINI

My favorite things to serve at my dinner parties are grissini (bread sticks) and crackers. I think it's because my guests love the crunchiness and the crazy shapes. This is a very artistic recipe, so go ahead and test your art!

INGREDIENTS

Basic Pizza Dough (see page 82)

4 tablespoons chopped rosemary

4 tablespoons finely chopped olives

2 tablespoons cracked pepper

4 tablespoons Parmigiano-Reggiano cheese

Olive oil, to taste

Sea salt, to taste

FACT: Crackers were invented by an American baker. They were so popular with sailors because they stayed crunchy through long travels. They were called sea biscuits.

DIRECTIONS

Preheat the oven to 400°F.

Follow the Basic Pizza Dough recipe, but don't let it sit for 20 minutes; use as soon as you're done kneading. Divide it into 4 parts. Add one of the other ingredients (rosemary, olives, pepper, and cheese) per part. Knead well.

To make the grissini: Make "snakes" or any shape you like with the dough.

To make the crackers: Using a rolling pin or pasta machine, roll the dough very thin. Cut into large rectangles or cracker shapes.

Place the crackers or grissini on a greased cookie sheet, brush with the oil, sprinkle with the salt, and bake until they start to brown (around 8 minutes for the crackers and 12 minutes for the grissini, depending on thickness).

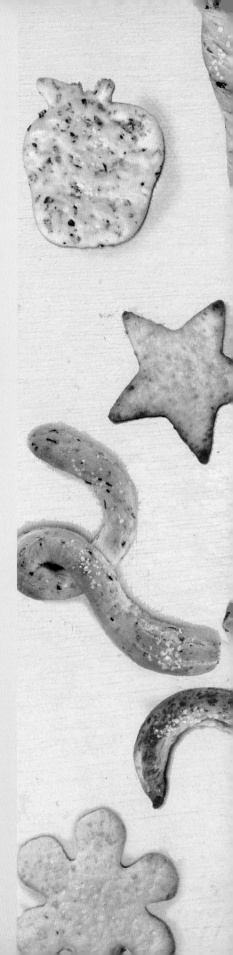

FO-KA-CHA <--Bless you

AKA FOCACCIA

In Parma, we call this torta salata (salted cake), and like a cake, it is fluffy and sweet on the inside but has coarse salt and olive oil on the crust. When it's still warm from the oven and filled with mortadella, it's the best thing I can think of! It reminds me of my childhood, when focaccia and mortadella was my favorite snack to take to school (Italians eat very little at breakfast so they need a snack midmorning).

INGREDIENTS

1 package or 2¼ teaspoons active dry yeast

1 teaspoon sugar

1 cup warm water (between 100°F and 110°F so you don't kill, or chill, the yeast)

9 tablespoons olive oil

2–3 cups all-purpose or whole wheat flour

1 teaspoon salt

1 teaspoon kosher salt

1 sprig rosemary, leaves removed (discard stem)

DIRECTIONS

Preheat the oven to 425°F.

Combine the yeast and sugar in a large bowl. Add the water and let sit for 5 minutes. Add 5 tablespoons of the oil and stir well. Add the flour to the bowl in small amounts and stir well after each addition. Halfway through the process of adding the flour, add the regular salt. The difference when you are making focaccia rather than pizza dough is that the dough has to be a little stickier than the pizza dough, almost a batter. Using your hands, knead the dough for 2 to 3 minutes on a lightly floured surface. Coat the dough with 1 tablespoon of the oil. Let the dough rest 30 minutes before using.

Grease a pan with 2 tablespoons of the olive oil. Spread the dough on the pan. Let it sit for another 30 minutes. With a fork, punch holes throughout the dough. Then sprinkle the remaining 1 tablespoon of olive oil all over the dough. Sprinkle with the kosher salt and rosemary. Bake for 20 to 25 minutes, or until lightly browned.

WHY NOTS
AKA GARLIC KNOTS

This is more like an American Italian recipe—but who cares? They are delicious!

INGREDIENTS

Basic Pizza Dough
(see page 82)

2 tablespoons olive oil

4 tablespoons butter

4 cloves garlic, peeled
and minced

4 tablespoons chopped
parsley

Kosher salt, to taste

DIRECTIONS

Preheat the oven to 400°F.

Roll the dough to 1 inch thick and cut into strips 1 inch wide and 4 inches long. Make a knot with the dough and place on a baking sheet covered with parchment paper. Brush the knots with the oil and cover with plastic wrap loosely; let rise until they double in size.

Place the baking sheet in the oven and bake for around 15 to 18 minutes until brown.

In the meantime, in a small skillet over medium heat, sauté the butter, garlic, and parsley for a few minutes, or until lightly browned. Remove from the heat and brush the knots with the mixture. Sprinkle with the salt. Serve immediately.

PIZZA S'MORE

AKA DESSERT PIZZA WITH CHOCOLATE AND MARSHMALLOWS

I've invented a pizza that bridges Italian and American culture! Please don't thank me, but maybe just vote for me: Chef Gino for president?

INGREDIENTS

1 tablespoon olive oil

Basic Pizza Dough (see page 82)

2 cups chocolate chips

1 cup mini marshmallows

DIRECTIONS

Preheat the oven to 400°F.

Grease a baking dish with the oil and spread the dough in it. Bake until brown for approximately 15 minutes. Take the pizza out of the oven and let it cool.

In a double boiler over high heat, melt the chocolate chips, stirring frequently. Remove from the heat when liquid. Spread the melted chocolate (you can also use hazelnut spread) on the dough evenly. Sprinkle with the marshmallows. Put under the broiler on high for 3 to 4 minutes, or until the marshmallows melt a little.

91

PIZZA BOWL AKA BACON AND EGGS PIZZA

When I think of this recipe, I think of my old friend Noah. He loved this pizza so much that I promised him I would mention him in my book if I was going to include the recipe. See, Noah? Chef Gino always keeps his promises!

INGREDIENTS

Basic Pizza Dough (see page 82)

4 slices cooked bacon

1 cup shredded Cheddar cheese

4 eggs

Salt and pepper, to taste

DIRECTIONS

Preheat the oven to 400°F.

Use a pizza cutter to carve 4 equal-size circles out of the dough (see the picture).

Oil a baking dish and put the 4 circles of dough in it. Bake until almost completely cooked, approximately 12 minutes.

Take out of the oven. Break the pieces of bacon and place evenly in the middle of the pizzas. Divide the cheese evenly on top of the bacon. Break 1 egg per pizza on top of the bacon and cheese.

Put back in the oven for 5 minutes. Finish under the broiler until preferred doneness of the egg is achieved. Sprinkle with the salt and pepper and serve.

FACT:
There are other kinds of eggs you can eat apart from the more familiar chicken eggs—quail, goose, turkey, emu, and even ostrich!

TAKE A DIP
AKA VEGETABLE DIPS

This is where I really want to challenge your taste. These little dips are perfect for grissini, crackers, or veggie sticks—but I'm sure you can come up with other options!

Eggplant Dip

INGREDIENTS

1 medium eggplant

1 clove garlic, peeled

4 tablespoons olive oil

2 leaves basil

Salt to taste

DIRECTIONS

Preheat the oven to 350°F.

Poke holes in the eggplant with a fork. Put directly on a rack in the oven for approximately 40 minutes, or until a fork inserts into the eggplant easily.

Remove from the oven and let the eggplant cool. When cool, peel the skin off. Put in a blender with the garlic, oil, basil, and salt. Blend and enjoy!

Artichoke Dip

INGREDIENTS

1 can artichokes, drained

½ cup canned cannellini beans, drained

1 tablespoon olive oil

1 tablespoon chopped parsley

Salt to taste

1 teaspoon lemon peel

DIRECTIONS

Put all the ingredients in a blender. Blend and enjoy!

PIZZA TOPPINGS MATRIX

There are two basic kinds of pizza: pizza rossa (red) with tomato sauce and pizza bianca (white) without tomato sauce. Test your taste with this matrix of ingredients that works for both.

1 VEGGIES	**2** MEAT OR FISH	**3** CHEESE	**4** HERBS & SPICES
olives	ham	Cheddar cheese	basil
mushrooms	pork sausage	mozzarella cheese	oregano
sliced bell peppers	shrimp	fontina cheese	crushed red pepper
sliced zucchini	bacon bits	burrata cheese	thyme
canned artichokes	anchovies	blue cheese	marjoram
cooked spinach	sliced smoked salmon		
fresh tomatoes			
pesto			
jalapeño			

CORN TORTILLAS

In case it wasn't clear yet—I am Italian but I have lived in Los Angeles for the last 25 years, so I know and appreciate Mexican food. Yes, I know, it may sound strange, but remember: Southern California used to be part of Mexico until 1848, so we know our Mexican food down here!

This chapter is all about corn tortillas. A tortilla is a wonderful flatbread made by combining flour and water. That's it? Well—no! Even though in Mexico they are used mostly as a substitute for bread, tortillas are the canvas for so many Mexican and Tex-Mex recipes.

BASIC TORTILLA

Making corn tortillas is just loco easy! You really only need two ingredients: corn flour and water (and a pinch of salt if you'd like—what's life without a little salt, right?). The flour you need is masa harina. This is a corn-based flour treated to soften the corn. You can find it in most well-stocked supermarkets, and you can't miss it in Mexican stores. Beware: Don't use cornmeal—it just won't work! Makes 20 tortillas (6-inches diameter).

INGREDIENTS

2 cups masa harina flour

Pinch of salt

1½ cups warm water

DIRECTIONS

To make the tortilla dough:

In a large bowl, combine the flour, salt, and water. Mix with a spoon. Use your hands to make a soft, pliable dough. Add a little water if the dough is too crumbly or a little masa if it's too sticky. Make 1 big ball with the dough, wrap it in plastic wrap, and put it in the refrigerator for 30 minutes. Take the dough out of the refrigerator, and make a big tube with the circumference of a golf ball. Using a butter knife, cut the tube in half, and keep cutting the half in half until you make 20 disks of dough. Roll the disks into balls approximately the size of golf balls.

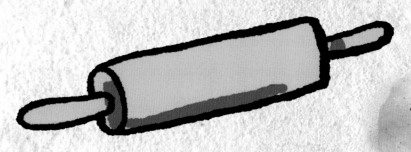

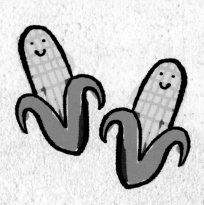

To roll the tortillas:

Start by trimming the side edges of a plastic sandwich bag (at least 6 inches wide) so that it's just like 2 pieces of plastic seamed at the base. Putting the dough inside the sandwich bag helps you make sure that the dough doesn't stick to the tortilla press or rolling pin. For extra no-stick action, you can brush a little vegetable oil on the inside of the bag before making your tortillas. To flatten your dough into a tortilla, you can use a tortilla press or a rolling pin.

If you're using a tortilla press: Take 1 ball at a time, put it inside the middle of the plastic bag, and place it all inside the tortilla press. Push the dough gently down with the palm of your hand, making sure it's wrapped in the plastic bag, and push the press's handle down.

If you're using a rolling pin: Put the ball of dough inside the sandwich bag and roll it with a rolling pin.

Once you've pressed the balls into flat disks approximately 6 inches in diameter, have a grown-up help you cook them.

To cook the tortillas:

Place 1 tortilla in a large skillet brushed with a small amount of vegetable oil over medium heat and cook each side for 2 to 3 minutes, being careful not to let them burn. Repeat the process for the 20 tortillas.

To store the tortillas:

Cover a shallow bowl with a tea towel and place your tortillas on it. Cover the tortillas with the edges of the towel. Keeping the tortillas inside the tea towel will keep them warm and soft—and yummy!

ZUCCADILLAS

AKA ZUCCHINI AND CHEESE QUESADILLAS

Quesadilla is the Mexican cousin of the grilled cheese sandwich. Everybody loves quesadillas! You just put cheese between two tortillas, then you bake them or put them in a skillet till the cheese melts—that's it! But sometimes if you want something more than a cheese quesadilla, you could try putting cooked vegetables in it, chicken, even ham! It's your quesadilla, so you do it the way you want! In my recipe, the Zuccadillas (can you pronounce it?), I use raw zucchini. But the zucchini are sliced so thin that they cook as the cheese melts. Makes 4 quesadillas.

INGREDIENTS

8 corn tortillas (page 98)

2 cups shredded cheese (mozzarella or Cheddar will do, but for a more original flavor, try to find the Mexican queso Oaxaca)

2 medium zucchini

Salt and pepper, to taste

DIRECTIONS

Preheat the oven to 350°F.

Place 4 tortillas side by side on a baking sheet. Sprinkle ½ cup of the cheese over each tortilla.

Take a peeler and peel the zucchini, making long thin strips of zucchini. Lay the zucchini strips evenly over each tortilla. Add the salt and pepper.

Cover the tortillas with the remaining 4 tortillas, and place the baking sheet in the oven for 6 to 7 minutes, or until the cheese is completely melted. Pile the 4 quesadillas up for a quadruple-decker tower of Zuccadillas!

BEWARE:

Melted cheese is super hot—so you'll have to be patient before eating your quesadillas. Once they cool off a little, you can fold a quesadilla in half and eat it like a sandwich or you can use a pizza cutter and cut it into 4 quarters.

TACO NIGHT
AKA TACOS WITH GROUND TURKEY

We love taco night at my house. We make a bunch of fresh corn tortillas (see page 98 for the recipe), or we buy corn or flour tortillas at the local Mexican market, and sometimes we even use hard-shell tortillas for extra crunch! The beauty of tacos is that the fillings are endless! You can have shrimp tacos if you want, roasted vegetables, bell peppers, steak tacos. Do you like it a little spicy? Add some jalapeño. You don't like lettuce? Then don't put in it, but the question is: Why don't you like lettuce?!

INGREDIENTS

1 tablespoon olive oil

½ pound ground turkey

   Salt and pepper, to taste

   Taco seasoning, to taste

8 corn tortillas (page 98)

1 medium onion, finely chopped

2 cups shredded lettuce

¼ cup sour cream

1 cup shredded cheese (mozzarella or Cheddar will do, but for a more original flavor, try to find the Mexican queso Oaxaca)

⅓ cup chopped cilantro

½ cup diced tomatoes

1 cup Beak of the Rooster (page 106)

1 cup Guac Amore (page 107)

DIRECTIONS

To make the ground turkey: Heat a medium skillet over medium heat. Add the oil and cook the ground turkey throughout until it is not pink. Add the salt and pepper and taco seasoning if you like it. Place in a large bowl for serving.

To make the tacos: Put all the ingredients out, grab a tortilla, and load it up with your favorite fillings. There's no right way or wrong way! Just *your* way! Fold the tortilla in half, and you have a taco. No silverware required!

FACT:

If you add live bacteria to cream, you have the process of souring—creating the sour cream!

CHIPILLAS

AKA TORTILLA CHIPS

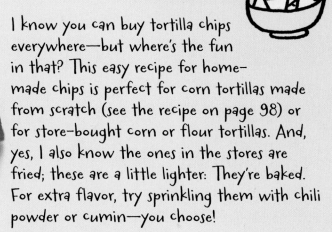

I know you can buy tortilla chips everywhere—but where's the fun in that? This easy recipe for home-made chips is perfect for corn tortillas made from scratch (see the recipe on page 98) or for store-bought corn or flour tortillas. And, yes, I also know the ones in the stores are fried; these are a little lighter: They're baked. For extra flavor, try sprinkling them with chili powder or cumin—you choose!

INGREDIENTS

8 corn tortillas (page 98)

½ cup vegetable oil

Kosher salt, to taste

DIRECTIONS

Preheat the oven to 400°F.

Brush each side of the tortillas with the oil. Take the tortillas and cut them in slices, or you can use cookie cutters and make them the shapes *you* like. Place the tortilla pieces in a single layer on a baking sheet. Sprinkle with the salt.

Place in the oven and bake for approximately 10 minutes, or until slightly brown but not burned! Serve with salsa and/or guacamole (see the recipes on pages 106 and 107).

CHEESY CHICK 'N' CHIPS

AKA CHICKEN NACHOS

Nachos are probably more Tex-Mex than Mexican, but they are so good and so easy to do—so who cares where they come from? The concept is very simple: You just take some tortilla chips, mix them with yummy stuff, top with cheese, and put in the oven until the cheese melts. Then scoop the cheesy chips with all the yummy stuff inside and enjoy. In this recipe, you can substitute the sour cream with a little Greek yogurt for a lighter flavor, and you can substitute all my ingredients with whatever you like.

INGREDIENTS

6–8 cups Chipillas (page 102)

1 cup drained black beans

1 cup shredded cooked chicken

1 cup shredded cheese (mozzarella or Cheddar will do, but for a more original flavor, try to find the Mexican queso Oaxaca)

1 avocado, peeled and diced

1 cup Beak of the Rooster (page 106)

½ cup sour cream

DIRECTIONS

Preheat the oven to 350°F.

Place the chips in a small lasagna pan, or make a pan out of foil. Mix them with the beans and chicken. Sprinkle the cheese on top and put in the oven until the cheese is melted, just a few minutes.

Take the pan out of the oven and top it all with the avocado, salsa, and sour cream.

TOSTADINES

AKA MINI TOSTADA SALADS WITH SHRIMP

Tostada in Spanish means "toasted"—but the tortilla used as a base for the recipe is actually traditionally fried. Go figure! But we are not going to toast or fry our tortillas to make our mini tostada salads; we're just going to bake them into a crunchy bowl, which we'll fill with a super-fresh shrimp salad. I'm hungry already.

INGREDIENTS

4 corn tortillas (page 98)

1 tablespoon vegetable oil

2 cups shredded lettuce

1 cup diced tomato

1 cup diced bell pepper

1 cup cooked shrimp

Salt and pepper, to taste

Juice of 1 lime

1 cup Beak of the Rooster (page 106)

1 cup chopped cilantro

DIRECTIONS

To make the tostada bowls:

The only way to make these bowls right is to use *warm* tortillas. So I recommend warming them up in a skillet or the oven before using them. Preheat the oven to 375°F. Take a muffin tin and flip it upside down. Brush it with the oil. Nestle the 4 tortillas between the empty spaces in the tin. Bake for 13 minutes, or until the tortillas are brown at the edges but not burned! Take them out of the oven and let cool.

To make the salad:

Put the lettuce, tomato, bell pepper, and shrimp in a bowl. Add the salt and pepper and lime juice and mix well. Once the tostada bowls are cooled, divide the salad among the tostada bowls. Top them with the salsa and cilantro.

FACT:

There are more than 100 kinds of shrimp. Some live to be 6 years old. An average shrimp has 10 legs!

BEAK OF THE ROOSTER

AKA SALSA FRESCA

"Beak of the rooster" is the English translation for pico de gallo, the Mexican name for a salsa made with fresh ingredients, perfect for tacos, burritos, and tortilla chips.

INGREDIENTS

1 large tomato

½ onion

Juice of ½ lime

2–4 cilantro leaves

Salt and pepper, to taste

1 jalapeño pepper, seeds removed and chopped, for a spicier salsa (optional); use gloves and have a grown-up help with this one

DIRECTIONS

Halve and seed the tomato and discard the seeds. Put all the ingredients in a blender and press the pulse button a few times. The salsa should be finely chopped but not liquid. Put in the refrigerator for 30 minutes before serving.

GUAC AMORE

AKA GUACAMOLE

I love guacamole. Who doesn't? Simple and fun to make, it's a great side for all your Mexican dishes!

INGREDIENTS

1 ripe avocado

½ tomato, halved and seeded

½ small onion, chopped

10–20 leaves cilantro, chopped

Juice of ½ lime

Salt and pepper, to taste

DIRECTIONS

Halve and pit the avocado. Spoon the flesh into a medium bowl. Add all the other ingredients and start mashing using a potato masher, fork, or a pestle. You can also use a blender—but come on! Where's the fun?

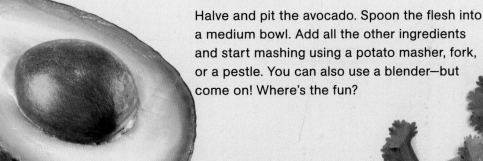

107

RANCHEGGOS

AKA HUEVOS RANCHEROS

How many times have you said: "Mom! Fried eggs again for breakfast?! Boring!"? These eggs are easy to make, and they give your everyday breakfast a Mexican flavor.

INGREDIENTS

4 corn tortillas (page 98)

1 tablespoon olive oil

4 large eggs

Salt and pepper, to taste

1 cup Beak of the Rooster (page 106)

1 avocado, peeled and sliced

DIRECTIONS

Preheat the oven to 350°F.

Place the tortillas on a baking sheet and put in the oven for 5 minutes, or until they are crisp but not burned.

In a medium skillet over medium heat, add the oil and fry the eggs to your taste and softness preference. Season with the salt and pepper.

Take the tortillas out of the oven, place on individual plates, place a fried egg on top of every tortilla, and scoop the salsa on each. Divide the avocado evenly among the eggs and enjoy!

MEXICAN SWEET TREATS

AKA CINNAMON AND SUGAR CRISPY TORTILLAS

This is a fun recipe. It looks like you're having tortilla chips and salsa, but you're really having dessert! Maybe instead of making the strawberry sauce, you could make a sweet guacamole—sweet guacamole? That's a great idea. How would you do it?

INGREDIENTS

Tortilla Chips

- 4 corn tortillas (page 98)
- ⅓ cup melted butter
- 2 tablespoons brown sugar, packed
- 1 tablespoon cinnamon

Strawberry Salsa

- 1 tablespoon butter
- 1 cup sliced strawberries
- 2 tablespoons brown sugar, packed

DIRECTIONS

To make the tortilla chips:

Preheat the oven to 350°F. Cut the tortillas into triangles, or use your favorite cookie cutters. Spread the tortilla pieces on a baking sheet in a single layer. Brush them with the butter. In a small bowl, mix together the sugar and cinnamon and sprinkle evenly on the tortilla pieces. Bake for approximately 10 minutes, or until brown but not burned!

To make the strawberry salsa:

Melt the butter in a small skillet over medium heat. Add the strawberries and sugar and cook for 5 to 6 minutes, stirring occasionally.

Serve the tortilla chips with the strawberry salsa while it's still warm.

MASH

To mash or not to mash—well, I love to mash! Give me a masher, a ricer, or even a fork and the fun begins. Come on, kids, admit it! You like it, too; it's not often that your parent would ask you to s-mash something, so take advantage of that and have fun.

TASTY TATOES

AKA MASHED POTATOES

Who doesn't like mashed potatoes? In Italy, we call it puré, from the word puree, I guess, and we do use the ricer. Why? Because it's fun!

INGREDIENTS

4 medium russet potatoes, peeled and cubed

4 tablespoons butter

¼ cup heavy cream

2 teaspoons salt

DIRECTIONS

Boil the potatoes in a large pot filled with water (about 2 quarts) over high heat until they can be easily skewered with a fork, approximately 30 minutes.

Drain the potatoes and add to a large bowl along with the butter, cream, and salt. Mash with a fork or a masher until there are no large clumps and then whisk until smooth. Serve warm.

FACT:

Potatoes are vegetables, but they contain a lot of starch, making them more like pasta or rice in terms of nutritional value. They also have very little sodium, which means that without a little salt, they are not very flavorful.

SMASHED SQUASH

AKA MASHED APPLE AND BUTTERNUT SQUASH

This is a recipe perfect for fall—but if you like butternut squash and apples, well, then it's perfect for the whole year round!

INGREDIENTS

2 apples, peeled, cored, and sliced

1 butternut squash, halved lengthwise, peeled, and cubed (discard seeds)

Salt and pepper, to taste

4 tablespoons butter

1 teaspoon cinnamon

½ teaspoon salt

DIRECTIONS

Preheat the oven to 375°F.

Spread out the apples and squash on a baking sheet. Sprinkle with the salt and pepper. Allow to roast for 30 minutes, or until golden and soft.

Remove from the oven. Spoon out the soft squash and apple slices into a medium bowl. Add the butter, cinnamon, and salt and mash until combined. Serve warm.

113

THUMBPRINTS
AKA GNOCCHI

Gnocchi! Gnocchi, more than a single recipe, is in fact a preparation. You can make gnocchi with cheese or leftover bread or spinach—the recipe in here is the most common: potato gnocchi. Did you know that something simple in Italy is defined as something gnocco? That's because gnocchi are so easy to make. Just make sure you get the right ratio of liquid and flour. One of the first memories I have in a kitchen is helping my mom making gnocchi. Having small fingers at the time, my job was to imprint my thumb in every nugget so that there would be a little space for the sauce to land.

INGREDIENTS

1 medium russet potato

½ cup flour (possibly more according to the starchiness of the potato)

1 egg yolk

2 pinches of salt

DIRECTIONS

Boil the potato in a large pot filled with at least 4 cups of water over high heat until it can be easily skewered with a fork, approximately 30 minutes. Drain the potato and let it sit until cool enough to handle but still warm. Peel it and mash with a ricer or masher or fork.

Make a well in the mashed potato in a large bowl or on a working surface. Mix in the flour, egg, and a pinch of the salt and knead with your hands until it is a pliable dough, adding more flour if too wet. Make a long tube the size of a nickel in diameter, and using a butter knife, cut the tube in approximately 1-inch nuggets. Push the nuggets gently down using the back of a fork (see the picture).

In a large heavy-bottom pot, bring 4 to 5 cups of water and a pinch of the salt to a boil over high heat. Have a grown-up help you carefully add the gnocchi to the boiling water. Cook for a few minutes. When the gnocchi come to the surface, they are ready and you can pick them up with a slotted spoon. Add to your favorite sauce or use the Pasta Sauce Matrix on page 44.

FACT:

The word gnocchi—it's hard to pronounce for American kids because of the gn sound in it. Think of lasagna or my last name Campagna.

114

Mash the cooked potato with a ricer or fork.

Make a well and pour in the flour, egg yolk, and salt.

Mix together with a fork or your hands.

Add more flour if necessary.

Use your hands to create a long tube with the dough.

Cut the tube into 1-inch nuggets.

Flatten the nuggets slightly with the back of a fork or your thumb.

Ready to add to the boiling water!

CARROT CRUSH

AKA MASHED CARROT WITH CUMIN

There's something about the combination of carrots and cumin that I love! Try to make this recipe using different colored carrots; the orange ones are fine—but what if you could find yellow carrots? Or purple? Ask at your local market!

INGREDIENTS

6 medium carrots, peeled

2 tablespoons butter

Cumin, to taste

Salt and pepper, to taste

DIRECTIONS

In a double boiler, steam the carrots over medium heat till very soft (you could also boil them). Transfer the carrots to a large bowl, add the rest of the ingredients, and mash with a masher until smooth.

FACT:

The seeds of the cumin plant make the spice we know as cumin. Did you know that cumin is present in most curry and chili powders? Now you do! Only black pepper is a more popular spice than cumin!

GOOEY TUNA

AKA CANNELLINI, AVOCADO, AND TUNA MASH

This is a great recipe for a snack or lunch. The cannellini beans and avocado make the "glue" to keep the tuna together. The more you mash, the smoother the mix will be. Mash away!

INGREDIENTS

½ can (7.5 ounces) cannellini beans, drained

1 large ripe avocado, peeled and chopped

1 can tuna, drained

4 spring onions, chopped

8–10 leaves parsley, chopped

Lemon zest

Salt and pepper, to taste

DIRECTIONS

Mash all the ingredients together in a large bowl and make a paste—perfect for a sandwich or dip.

FLOWER MASH

AKA CURRY CAULIFLOWER MASH

Come on, I know! Curry is not a Mediterranean flavor, and I sure didn't even know it existed when I was growing up. But it's such a powerful spice that I had to include it in at least one recipe. Combined with cauliflower, it's one of my favorite flavors!

INGREDIENTS

4 tablespoons vegetable oil

1 teaspoon cumin

1 teaspoon coriander

2 teaspoons turmeric

1 tablespoon chili powder

½ teaspoon ground ginger

3 cups cauliflower florets

2 cloves garlic, chopped

1 teaspoon salt

DIRECTIONS

Preheat the oven to 350°F.

In a medium skillet over medium-high heat, warm 2 tablespoons of the oil. Add the cumin, coriander, turmeric, chili powder, and ginger and brown for 1 minute. Add the cauliflower, garlic, and salt and toss for 3 minutes, or until completely covered.

Turn the cauliflower onto a baking sheet greased with the remaining 2 tablespoons oil and place in the oven. Allow to roast for 25 to 30 minutes, or until golden and soft. Remove from the oven and allow to rest until completely cool.

Put the cauliflower into a large bowl and mash until it forms a soft paste using a fork or masher (you can also use a food processor). Serve warm or cold—it's good both ways!

FACT:

There are many different varieties of cauliflower. I know the most common is the white one, but look carefully next time you shop at a supermarket or your local farmers' market, and you can find orange, green, and even purple ones!

APPLESAUCE

Try to experiment with different kinds of apples and different spices. It's the perfect simple recipe to challenge your taste!

INGREDIENTS

½ cup water

4 apples, cored and diced

1 tablespoon lemon juice

¼ cup brown sugar, packed

Cinnamon, to taste (optional)

DIRECTIONS

In a large saucepan, mix the water with the apples, lemon juice, and sugar. Cook at low heat for around 30 minutes, or until the apples get the consistency of—applesauce! Add cinnamon if you like.

FRUIT SAUCE

INGREDIENTS

2 tablespoons butter

2 cups raspberries

2 tablespoons sugar

DIRECTIONS

In a large saucepan over medium heat, melt the butter and add the berries and sugar. Stir and cook till the fruit is a mush!

NOTE: You can substitute the raspberries with straw-berries, blueberries, peaches, bananas, or any combi-nations of these. Use the sauce to top pancakes, waffles, ice cream, or even hot and cold cereals.

BANACAKES

AKA BANANA-EGG PANCAKES

This is a great little recipe for those bananas left out for a few days. Don't be afraid of bananas that are turning black! The darker they get, the sweeter they are!

INGREDIENTS

2 large eggs

½ teaspoon baking powder

1 teaspoon vanilla extract

1 tablespoon sugar

Pinch of salt

2 very ripe bananas

3 tablespoons butter

DIRECTIONS

In a large bowl, beat the eggs. Add the baking powder, vanilla, sugar, and salt.

Mash the bananas in a medium bowl (leave some chunks), and add to the egg mixture and mix well.

Melt ½ tablespoon of the butter in a medium non-stick skillet and pour out the batter to make a pancake 4 to 5 inches in diameter. Cook till brown around the edges and then flip. Beware: The banana cakes are a little more delicate than regular pancakes, so be very gentle. Repeat until all the batter is used. Add ½ tablespoon of the butter to the skillet between cooking pancakes.

Serve with maple syrup or Fruit Sauce (page 119).

POTATO FINGERS

AKA LEFTOVER MASHED POTATO CHEESE TUBES

Do you have some mashed potatoes left over from yesterday? Try this simple recipe that reminds me of classic Italian street food: hot and delicious!

INGREDIENTS

2 cups leftover Tasty Tatoes (page 112)

½ cup diced ham

½ cup shredded mozzarella cheese

1 tablespoon chopped parsley

Salt and pepper, to taste

1 large egg

1 cup bread crumbs

DIRECTIONS

Preheat the oven to 350°F.

In a large bowl, combine the mashed potatoes with the ham, cheese, and parsley. Add the salt and pepper.

Beat the egg in a medium bowl with a pinch of salt. Place the bread crumbs on a plate.

Form small tubes with the potato mix the size of an adult's thumb. Roll them first in the egg and then in the bread crumbs. Place in an oiled baking dish and cook for 20 minutes.

NOTE: If you don't have leftover mashed potatoes, here's how to make them: Peel and boil the potatoes until soft, then mash them with a masher or ricer.

TOPPINGS AND SPICES FOR THE MASHES

Some of the recipes in this chapter can be—dare I say it?—
boring by themselves! I like to spice most of these mashes up with
some more flavors. Mix them however you want—but remember:
Find a balance!

bacon bits

chopped chives

sour cream

Greek yogurt

shredded Cheddar cheese

crumbled Gorgonzola cheese

chopped walnuts

cinnamon

Parmigiano-Reggiano cheese

chopped spring onions

red-pepper flakes

crumbled hard-boiled eggs

cumin

nutmeg

123

EGGS

Eggs! The perfect food, beautiful to look at and full of potential! Elegant and classy, and they form the bond for so many ingredients. I just think I could write a book about eggs, maybe more than one, never running out of recipes for this incredible ingredient.

You will see in this chapter that some recipes are pretty similar; after all, a frittata is like a quiche without the crust and with Parmigiano-Reggiano, and the omelet is like scrambled eggs that are not scrambled, more like a clafoutis (a baked fruit dessert) that is like a frittata that is like a quiche—well, you get the idea!

MINI QUICHES LORRAINE

FRANCE

Quiches are just fantastic! You can make quiche with pretty much anything you want. I love the ones with crust, and I love the ones without—but by now you should know: There's no food I don't love!

INGREDIENTS

1 recipe Pie Crust (see page 135)

½ cup crisply cooked and crumbled bacon

1 cup shredded Swiss or Cheddar cheese

⅓ cup finely chopped onion

4 large eggs

1½ cups whipping cream or whole milk

Salt and pepper, to taste

DIRECTIONS

Preheat the oven to 425°F.

With a floured rolling pin, roll the pie crust into 12 round pieces the size of the top of a muffin cup (we need to have little edges).

Place the pastry pieces in the muffin cups. Add the bacon, cheese, and onion evenly. Beat the eggs, cream or milk, and salt and pepper in a large bowl and pour gently into the cups. Cook for 20 minutes, or until set on top.

NOTE: You can do the same recipe without the pie crust and substituting the bacon with salmon; you will make a crustless quiche with salmon.

FACT:

Emmental cheese, or Swiss cheese as it's called in America, is known for its holes. The holes are created by bubbles of air left by the living bacteria used in the cheese-making process. The holes are called eyes. A Swiss cheese without holes is called blind!

VEGGIE WEDGIE

AKA MUSHROOM FRITTATA

My mom used to make this recipe using half the amount of Parmigiano-Reggiano and substituting it with bread crumbs. Nobody else I knew did it like that! It was only years later that I realized bread crumbs are cheaper than cheese.

INGREDIENTS

- 2 tablespoons olive oil
- 1 small onion, diced
- 1 cup diced mushrooms
- 4 medium eggs

- ½ cup grated Parmigiano-Reggiano cheese
- Salt and pepper, to taste
- 1 small bunch parsley, leaves removed and chopped

DIRECTIONS

In a large ovenproof skillet over medium-high heat, add the oil and sauté the onion and mushrooms for a few minutes till soft.

In the meantime, in a medium bowl, beat the eggs. Add the cheese and salt and pepper and mix well.

Pour the egg mixture into the skillet with the vegetables. Lower the heat to medium-low. Switch on the broiler, and after 4 or 5 minutes on the stove, take the skillet and put it in the broiler and cook the upper part of the frittata for another 5 to 6 minutes. Return to the stove for a few minutes to make sure the bottom is cooked. Sprinkle with the parsley and serve.

SCRAMBLER
AKA VEGGIE SCRAMBLED EGGS

The key to this recipe is the ingredients: I want colors—vibrant, beautiful colors swimming in the sea of scrambled eggs! (I feel like a poet today.)

INGREDIENTS

2 tablespoons olive oil

1 small onion, diced

½ cup diced mushrooms

½ cup diced bell peppers

½ cup diced zucchini

4 large eggs

½ cup milk or heavy cream

Salt and pepper, to taste

1 small bunch parsley, leaves removed and chopped

WISK

DIRECTIONS

In a medium skillet, add the oil and sauté the onion and all the other vegetables for a few minutes till soft.

In the meantime, in a medium bowl, beat the eggs (make sure you beat them for at least 3 minutes). Add the milk or cream and salt and pepper and mix well.

Pour the egg mixture into the skillet with the vegetables. Make sure you stir while cooking so that the eggs don't stick to the skillet. Sprinkle with the parsley once cooked to the desired consistency (I like mine soft) and serve.

EGGY FLIP
AKA OMELETS

This is a great breakfast item, but I used to eat it at dinner sometimes. When there was nothing else in the fridge, my mom could always find a few eggs and make an omelet. It requires a little bit of care in the preparation; you want to flip it in half without breaking it, and you want to make sure to flip it again before it burns. But once you've got it down (I made it sound way more difficult than it really is), you can make omelets for the rest of your life!

INGREDIENTS

2 tablespoons olive oil

¼ cup diced mushrooms

¼ cup diced bell peppers

¼ cup diced broccoli

8 large eggs

¼ cup milk

Salt and pepper, to taste

1 cup shredded mozzarella cheese

DIRECTIONS

In a large skillet over medium-high heat, add 1 tablespoon of the oil and sauté the vegetables for 2 to 3 minutes till soft.

In the meantime, in a large bowl, beat the eggs and milk. Add the salt and pepper.

Heat up the remaining 1 tablespoon oil in a nonstick skillet. Pour in a quarter of the egg mixture and let it cook at medium-low heat for a couple of minutes. Add a quarter of the vegetable mixture on top and ¼ cup of the cheese. When the omelet starts solidifying at the edges, fold half of it on the other half, closing the omelet. Let it cook for a couple of minutes, and then carefully flip the omelet and cook the other side for 3 to 4 minutes.

Repeat the process for more omelets!

129

ANGEL EGGS
AKA DEVILED EGGS

This is one of my favorite appetizers! I love hard-boiled eggs, and preparing them this way just makes them so much more fun! Serve them on a big platter; your friends will love them, and don't forget to invite me!

INGREDIENTS

6 hard-boiled eggs

1 tablespoon tomato paste or ketchup

Salt, to taste

1 tablespoon mayo

1 tablespoon Dijon mustard

10–15 leaves parsley, chopped

Paprika, to taste

FACT:

Dijon mustard is named after the city where it was created in France: Dijon. Here are other food items that take their names from the place they originated: balsamic vinegar of Modena, Philly cheesesteak, prosciutto di Parma, Peking (another name for the Chinese city of Beijing) duck, MoonPie—wait, the moon?

DIRECTIONS

Peel and cut the eggs lengthwise. Scoop the yolks from 2 of the eggs and put them in a small bowl. Mix the yolks with the tomato paste or ketchup and add the salt.

Put the mix in a pastry bag with a flower tip and squeeze the mix back in the 2 boiled eggs.

Repeat with the mayo and mustard.

Decorate the eggs with the parsley and sprinkle with the paprika.

HOW CAN YOU TELL IF AN EGG IS SUPER FRESH OR NOT?
Drop the raw egg in a bowl of water.

Fresh eggs will sink on their sides (too fresh for hard boiling).

Older eggs will sink at a tilted or upright position (perfect for hard-boiling).

If your egg floats, it's too old; don't use it!

CROQUE-MONSIEUR
AKA FRENCH TOAST GRILLED CHEESE

I know, I know, this is almost like a grilled cheese sandwich, but trust me when I tell you that when you're preparing a recipe, everything will sound better if you pronounce it in French, Italian, or Spanish (or Japanese, Chinese, Vietnamese, etc.).

INGREDIENTS

8 slices whole wheat bread

3 large eggs

Pinch of salt

2 cups shredded Swiss cheese

4 slices ham

2 cups bread crumbs

4 tablespoons butter

DIRECTIONS

Cut the crust off the bread. Beat the eggs with the salt in a medium bowl and dip a slice of the bread in the mixture. Remove the bread quickly and set on a plate or working surface. Place ½ cup of the cheese and 1 slice of the ham evenly on the bread. Take another slice of bread, dip it in the egg mixture, and place it on top of the other slice topped with ham and cheese. Take the sandwich and coat it with the bread crumbs.

Heat up a medium skillet over medium heat, melt 1 tablespoon of the butter, and place the sandwich in the skillet. Cook for 3 to 4 minutes per side, or until the bread crumbs are browned and the cheese is melted. Repeat for the other 3 sandwiches.

NOTE: You can also bake the sandwiches in the oven for 15 minutes at 350°F.

EASY CAKE
AKA SWEET CLAFOUTIS

This is the best dessert you can learn! There's no baking powder or baking soda, none of those difficult mixtures: No! This is sooooo simple, and it can be done with many different ingredients, so it's the perfect Chef Gino dessert. The traditional one is done with pitted cherries—to die for! You can always see in a pastry store which one is a clafoutis among all the desserts because of its characteristic gelatin-like texture.

INGREDIENTS

3 large eggs

½ cup sugar

½ cup flour

1 cup whole milk

1 teaspoon vanilla extract

Pinch of salt

2 cups berries of your choice

FACT:

There's a saying in Italy: Una ciliegia tira l'altra. That translates to "a cherry leads to another cherry." It means it's very hard to stop at just one cherry!

DIRECTIONS

Preheat the oven to 325°F.

In a medium bowl, beat the eggs with the sugar, slowly adding the flour. Slowly pour in the milk and keep mixing. Add the vanilla and salt and mix well.

Butter up a pie dish. Gently position the berries in the bottom and slowly pour the mix around them. Cook for 35 to 40 minutes, or until the top feels elastic to the touch.

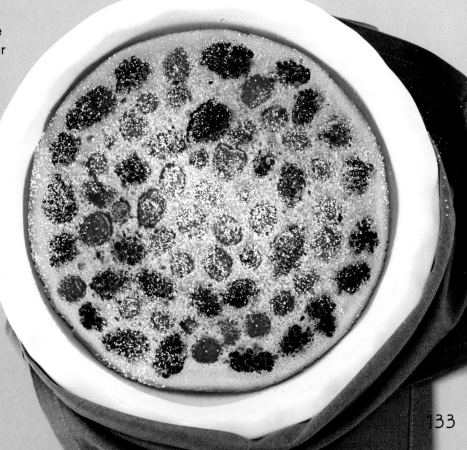

133

OUTSTANDING OVEN EGGS

AKA EGGS POACHED IN THE OVEN

There's something magical about the way poached eggs look: They look like they are suspended in space without their shell to protect them. This is a very simple recipe for making poached eggs to perfection!

INGREDIENTS

12 large eggs

DIRECTIONS

Preheat the oven to 350°F.

Pour 1 tablespoon of water in each cup of a muffin pan, and then gently crack the eggs into the cups. Bake for 13 to 15 minutes, or until the whites are set but the yolks are runny.

PIE CRUST

Well, this is one of those recipes that if you learn how to make it, you can make pies (sweet and savory) for the rest of your life! So—what are you waiting for? Makes 1 double-crust 9-inch or 10-inch pie.

INGREDIENTS

2½ cups flour

1 teaspoon salt

2 tablespoons sugar

1 cup (1½ sticks) unsalted butter, chilled and cut into ¼-inch cubes

6–8 tablespoons ice water

DIRECTIONS

In a medium bowl, mix the flour, salt, and sugar. Cut in the butter, using your hands or a fork until particles are the size of small peas. Sprinkle with the water, 1 tablespoon at a time, tossing with a fork until all the flour is moistened and the dough is smooth and not too sticky (1 to 2 teaspoons more water can be added if necessary).

Gather the pastry dough into a ball. Shape into a flattened round on a lightly floured surface and wrap in plastic. Refrigerate for about 45 minutes, or until the dough is firm and cold yet pliable.

Roll it according to recipes.

135

CREPES

The first thing I ever learned how to make professionally was crepes. At the time in Parma, they were an unusual, almost exotic recipe. In the small café where I was working at the time, they had the traditional large round burners and that little wooden spatula that helps you spread the mixture evenly: I loved crepes immediately. They are a staple at my house for breakfast or lunch, and sometimes they make a beautiful dessert. How will you make yours?

BASIC CREPES

You probably don't have the large burner they use in France to make the crepes, but no worries! All you need is a nonstick skillet around 6 inches in diameter and you'll be fine! Makes 8 crepes, using ¼ cup of mix per crepe.

INGREDIENTS

1 cup flour

2 large eggs

1½ cups milk

2 teaspoons vegetable oil

¼ teaspoon salt

DIRECTIONS

In a large bowl, whisk together the flour and eggs. Gradually add in the milk and oil, stirring to combine. Add the salt.

Heat a lightly oiled griddle or skillet over medium-high heat. Cook the crepe for about 2 minutes, or until the bottom is light brown. Flip it and cook for 2 minutes on the other side. Repeat the process until you use all of the crepe batter.

FACT:

Some recipes will call for strips of crepe to be added to a meat soup (like the Mighty Meat Broth on page 4), such as the Austrian frittatensuppe! Isn't that a great name?

Assemble your ingredients and add flour and eggs to a large bowl.

Slowly add in the milk and oil.

Cook the crepe for 2 minutes.

Flip it to the other side for another 2 minutes!

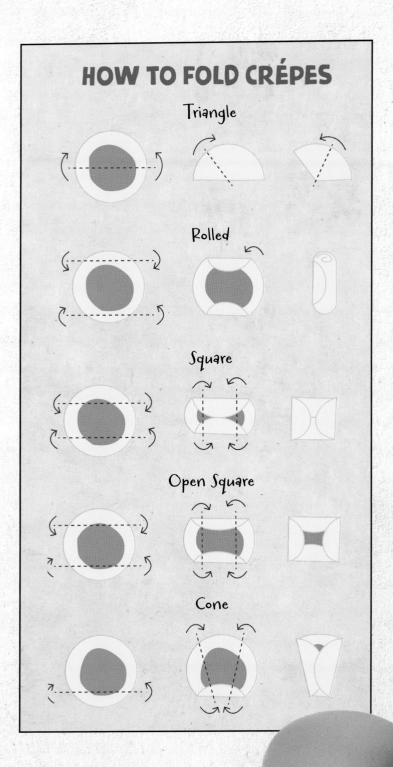

HOW TO FOLD CRÉPES

Triangle

Rolled

Square

Open Square

Cone

SWEET TREAT CREPES
AKA FOUR DIFFERENT SWEET CREPES

If you're ever in a classy French restaurant and you see crepes Suzette on the menu—go for it! If they do it right, they flame the crepes right in front of your eyes; unfortunately, flaming stuff is not really a good idea for you to make at home—but there are enough ideas in the following recipe to keep you busy for a while.

INGREDIENTS

- 4 Basic Crepes (page 138)
- 4 tablespoons butter
- 4 tablespoons confectioners' sugar
- 2 tablespoons honey
- ½ cup chopped walnuts
- 1 banana, sliced
- ½ cup shredded coconut
- ¼ cup hazelnut spread
- ½ cup sliced strawberries

DIRECTIONS

Preheat the oven to 350°F.

For the sweet crepe with butter and sugar: Spread 1 crepe on a plate. Sprinkle 2 tablespoons of the butter and 2 tablespoons of the sugar on it. Fold the crepe in half and then in half again; roll it, burrito-style; or fold it in half and then roll almost like a cone. Sprinkle with a little of the remaining sugar.

For the sweet crepe with honey and walnuts: Spread 1 crepe on a plate. Spread the honey on it and sprinkle with the walnuts. Fold (see the instructions and pictures on page 139) and sprinkle with a little of the remaining sugar.

For the sweet crepe with banana and coconut: Spread 1 crepe on a plate. Place the banana on it and sprinkle with the shredded coconut. Fold (see the instructions and pictures on page 139) and sprinkle with a little of the remaining sugar.

For the sweet crepe with hazelnut spread and strawberries: Spread 1 crepe on a plate. Spread the hazelnut spread on it and sprinkle with the strawberries. Fold (see the instructions and pictures on page 139) and sprinkle with a little of the remaining sugar.

Place the folded crepes in a buttered baking dish, and sprinkle with the remaining 2 tablespoons butter. Bake for 5 minutes, or until the butter is melted and browning on top of the crepes.

DON'T CRY!

FACT: According to ancient Egyptian legend, the Sun God was once so brokenhearted that he started to cry. His tears dripped on Earth in the form of honey! This is a lovely legend, but we all know that honey is made by our indispensable bees!

SAVORY ME A CREPE
AKA SAVORY CREPES

There's no end to the possibilities here. Savory crepes are perfect to challenge your taste. I just want to remind you that some cheese should always be included and that the meats and vegetables you use should be cooked beforehand, as you can't keep the crepe on a skillet for too long or it will dry out and eventually—burn!

INGREDIENTS

2 tablespoons butter

½ medium onion, diced

1 cup sliced champignon (button) mushrooms

1 cup shredded mozzarella cheese

1 cup diced cooked ham

Salt and pepper, to taste

4 Basic Crepes (page 138)

2 tablespoons grated Parmigiano-Reggiano cheese

DIRECTIONS

Preheat the oven to 350°F.

In a large skillet over medium-high heat, melt the butter and cook the onion and mushrooms for 3 to 4 minutes, or until cooked through. Let them cool, and then add the mozzarella and ham. Sprinkle with the salt and pepper.

One by one, fill the crepes evenly with the mixture and fold according to the instructions and pictures on page 139.

Place the crepes in a buttered baking dish, sprinkle with the Parmigiano-Reggiano, and put in the oven for 10 minutes, or until the cheese is melted on top.

CRESPELLE
AKA CREPE "NOODLES" WITH ZUCCHINI

How about crepes used like pasta? That's heaven to me!

INGREDIENTS

8 Basic Crepes (page 138)

1 tablespoon butter

½ small onion, diced

1 medium zucchini, thinly sliced

¼ cup cream

½ cup grated Parmigiano-Reggiano cheese

Salt and pepper, to taste

DIRECTIONS

Cut the crepes with cookie cutters the way you like them, or cut strips to resemble fettuccine. Set aside.

In a medium skillet over medium-high heat, melt the butter. Add the onion and after a few minutes add the zucchini. Cook until the zucchini is tender. Add the crespelle (the cut-up crepes). Mix and add the cream and cheese. Add the salt and pepper. Mix some more and serve.

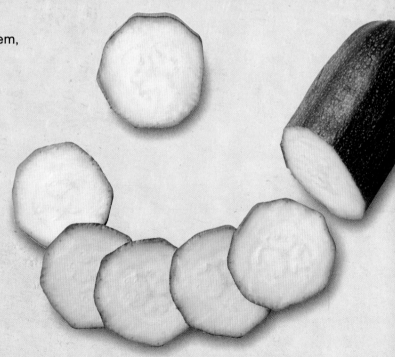

143

CREPELLONI

AKA "CANNELLONI" WITH RICOTTA CHEESE

Here is another recipe that uses crepes in place of pasta. But you know what? Sometimes crepes are faster to prepare, and they give the dish a richer flavor.

INGREDIENTS

1 cup fresh ricotta cheese

1 cup boiled and chopped spinach

1 cup grated Parmigiano-Reggiano cheese

1 cup shredded mozzarella

Salt and pepper, to taste

4 Basic Crepes (page 138)

1 tablespoon butter

Four Formaggi Sauce (page 149)

DIRECTIONS

Preheat the oven to 350°F.

Put the ricotta, spinach, half of the Parmigiano-Reggiano, the mozzarella, and the salt and pepper in a large bowl and mix well. Spread the filling evenly on the 4 crepes and roll the crepes onto themselves.

Grease a baking dish with the butter and lay the rolled-up crepes next to each other. Pour your favorite sauce (such as my Four Formaggi Sauce) over them and sprinkle with the remaining Parmigiano-Reggiano. Bake for 20 minutes.

CREPE NESTS
AKA FRUIT-FILLED CREPE BOWLS

You can't prepare this recipe too much in advance. I recommend preparing all the ingredients and assembling the recipe at the last moment: You don't want the fruit salad to make the crepe bowls soggy. But I'd still eat them!

INGREDIENTS

- 4 Basic Crepes (page 138)
- 4 cups Fruta Fresca (page 23)
- 4 cups vanilla ice cream or Greek yogurt

DIRECTIONS

Preheat the oven to 350°F.

Fold the crepes in half and form them into cups in a prepared muffin pan. Bake for 10 to 12 minutes, or until the crepes are slightly crispy. Remove from the oven and allow to cool on a rack.

Once they are at room temperature, fill them with the fruit salad and top with the ice cream or yogurt.

TOWER OF CREPES CAKE

AKA LAYER CREPE CAKE WITH HAZELNUT SPREAD

Don't want to bake but still want a cake? Try this tower of crepes—the more crepes you make, the taller the tower can be. Let me know how high you can go!

INGREDIENTS

- 12 ounces milk chocolate, chopped
- 1 cup toasted hazelnuts
- 2 tablespoons canola oil
- 1 tablespoon unsweetened cocoa powder
  Pinch of salt
- 1 cup whipping cream
- 3 tablespoons confectioners' sugar, plus more for dusting
- 10–12 Basic Crepes (page 138)
- 2 cups raspberries

DIRECTIONS

To make the hazelnut spread: Melt the chocolate in a double boiler over high heat, stirring occasionally. Remove from the heat once melted. In a food processor, grind the hazelnuts. Add the oil, cocoa powder, and salt and continue mixing till smooth. Add the melted chocolate and blend well. Let it cool and put in the refrigerator for at least 1 hour before using.

To make the whipped cream: In a large bowl, mix the cream with the sugar using a mixer on high. Mix till fluffy but not buttery.

Once the hazelnut spread is cold, start layering the crepes with a layer of spread till you have a tower of crepes filled with spread.

Leave the top crepe without spread.

Use a spreader to spread the whipped cream around on the top of the tower. Arrange the raspberries on top. Dust with the sugar.

Put in the refrigerator for an hour and serve.

MAPLE SYRUP CREPES

I think of this recipe as France meets America; the filling is savory, but the maple syrup in the crepes gives them a sweet aftertaste, a bit like when people pour maple syrup on their eggs and sausages.

INGREDIENTS

- 4 Basic Crepes (page 138, but substitute ¼ cup milk with maple syrup)
- 1 recipe Scrambler (page 128)
- 4 slices provolone cheese
- 4 slices ham

DIRECTIONS

Preheat the oven to 350°F.

Prepare the crepes and fill them with the eggs, cheese, and ham. Fold the crepes and place in a buttered baking dish. Cook for 10 minutes, or until the cheese is melted.

FACT:

My wife, Laura, always tells me how when she was little and living in Michigan, she would go and visit farmers in the winter. They would collect the sap of a maple tree, and then they would boil it in an open vat to make syrup. She said there was nothing more delicious than a spoonful of hot syrup over a ball of fresh snow! I love that story!

148

FOUR FORMAGGI SAUCE
AKA FOUR CHEESE SAUCE

This is a simple sauce that can be used in a variety of recipes. Be careful: When the cheese melts—it's hot! And there are four different types of cheese in this recipe, but what about three? Or six? It's up to you. A six-cheese sauce would be called sei formaggi!

INGREDIENTS

- ½ cup shredded mozzarella cheese
- ½ cup shredded Cheddar cheese
- ½ cup crumbled blue cheese
- 4 tablespoons butter
- 2 tablespoons cream
- 4 tablespoons grated Parmigiano-Reggiano cheese

DIRECTIONS

Put all the ingredients in a double boiler and melt the cheeses on medium heat until smooth. Stir occasionally. Use while warm.

150

FRUIT

Hi!

Ah, fruit! We call it frutta in Italy. Nowadays, you can find any kind of fruit you want at any time of the year, but when I was growing up, fruit was strictly a seasonal thing. Apples and pears were always available, but you could only taste cherries for a couple of months per year in the summer. There was something special in the anticipation of watermelon in late June and grapes in September. Now that you can find any fruit any time of the year, just remember that fruit is best when it's ripe. Stores these days tend to sell not-ripe fruits, so you have to be patient and let them ripen in a paper bag for a few days—that's when the flavor comes out.

BAKED PEARS

This is one of my favorite side dishes for Thanksgiving (but you don't have to wait for Turkey Day to make it). These pears go so well with meat, and they look so pretty. I also love the contrast between the savory meat and the sweetness of the pears.

INGREDIENTS

4 pears

2 tablespoons balsamic vinegar

4 tablespoons brown sugar

2 tablespoons maple syrup

DIRECTIONS

Preheat the oven to 375°F.

Take the pears and wash them, core them, and slice them in half lengthwise. Put them in a baking dish and sprinkle them evenly on top with the vinegar, then the sugar, and then the syrup. Cook for 40 minutes.

Eat hot or cold. They are great as a side dish for a roast.

FRUIT KEBABS

I've hosted a lot of cooking parties for kids in my life, possibly more than anybody else. I always introduce this recipe by saying: "This recipe is so simple—I'm ashamed of being a chef." What I mean is that there is really no right or wrong way to do this: Just be creative and eat all the leftovers!

INGREDIENTS

Fresh fruit, such as strawberries, grapes, bananas, melon, watermelon, and kiwifruit

Wooden skewers

Yogurt of your choice and shredded coconut for garnish

DIRECTIONS

Peel and chop the fruit if needed. Use your small cookie cutters when possible to shape the fruit. Then thread the pieces of fruit on the skewers. Sprinkle with the yogurt and coconut.

FACT: The banana tree is not a true fruit tree but a giant herb, and the banana is actually its berry. A banana plant produces only one bunch or "hand" in its life, but that bunch may have between 100 and 400 bananas.

153

SUMMER SLURPS
AKA FRUIT SMOOTHIES

This shouldn't even need explanation: I love smoothies! You get all the power of fruit in one delicious experience! There is really no right or wrong way to do this: Just have fun and be creative with the ingredients!

INGREDIENTS

Fresh fruit, such as bananas, melon, watermelon, kiwifruit, and berries

Plain yogurt or whole milk

Ice

DIRECTIONS

Peel and chop the fruit if needed. Put all the ingredients in a blender and have fun.

NOTE: You can also use frozen fruit, and then you don't need the ice!

FRUITY POPS

AKA FROZEN FRUIT AND YOGURT

This recipe is perfect for a hot summer day—who am I kidding? This recipe is always perfect! Remember, though, that if you can't find fresh seasonal fruit, you can still make this recipe by using frozen fruit.

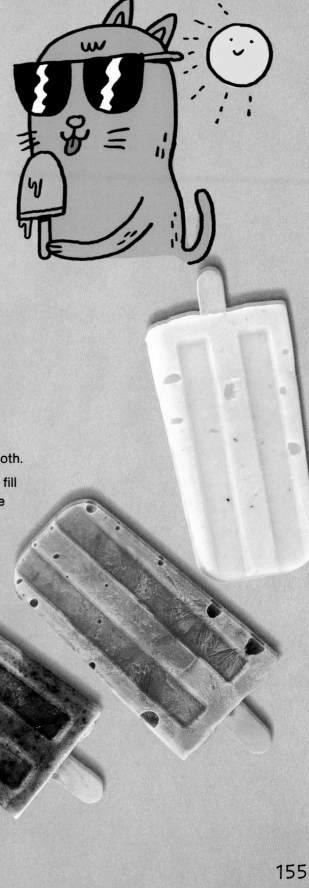

INGREDIENTS

- 2 cups mixed fresh fruit (blueberries, blackberries, bananas, strawberries, and raspberries are ideal)
- 2 cups plain or vanilla Greek yogurt
- 3 tablespoons honey
- 2 tablespoons lemon juice

DIRECTIONS

Put all the ingredients in a blender and mix until everything is smooth.

Take small paper cups (if you want mini pops, use Dixie cups) and fill them up three-quarters of the way with the fruit mixture. Cover the tops with aluminum foil and place a small wooden stick through each one. For the Dixie cups, you can also use a wooden pick.

Freeze for at least 5 hours. When you are ready to enjoy your pops, prepare a cereal bowl filled with hot water. Dip the pops still in the cups in the hot water (don't submerge) for 5 to 10 seconds. Your pops should come out real easy now!

WATERMELON SALAD

Nothing says summer to my family more than this recipe. I love to grill, and I love to shock my guests by saying that I will grill—a watermelon! This is a simple but super-delicious recipe that also looks fantastic!

INGREDIENTS

- 4 watermelon "patties" (1 inch thick and 4 inches in diameter; use a round cookie cutter or knife)
- 4 cups arugula
- 1 cup dried cranberries
- 1 cup feta cheese
- 1 cup caramelized pecans
- 4 tablespoons olive oil
- 2 tablespoons freshly squeezed lemon juice
- Salt and pepper, to taste

DIRECTIONS

Preheat a grill to medium or a grill pan over high heat.

Grill the watermelon patties, 2 minutes per side.

Prepare the salad by tossing all the other ingredients in a large bowl. Serve by scooping the salad evenly over the watermelon patties.

FACT:

All parts of the watermelon are edible. But because it doesn't taste so good, the rind is not usually eaten—except in China, where it's used as a vegetable and stir-fried, stewed, and pickled!

DIP IT GOOD!
AKA GREEK YOGURT DIP FOR FRUIT

How can we possibly make fruit more delicious? If you really want to try, you can start with this simple dip for fruit and see how it works.

INGREDIENTS

½ cup plain Greek yogurt

1 tablespoon freshly squeezed orange juice

1 teaspoon honey

½ cup raspberries or blackberries

2 tablespoons shredded coconut

DIRECTIONS

In a small bowl, mix the yogurt, orange juice, and honey. With a spoon, push the berries through a fine-mesh strainer or sieve so that the juice of the berries goes in the yogurt mix and the seeds stay in the strainer. Mix and sprinkle the coconut on top for decoration. Dip away!

BANANA HALF-SPLIT
AKA YOGURT-TOPPED FRUIT

Well, yes, I love banana splits! This one is on the lighter side because it uses Greek yogurt instead of ice cream—so you can enjoy it a little more often.

INGREDIENTS

4 bananas

4 cups fruit-flavored Greek yogurt

1 cup nuts, such as peanuts or cashews

1 cup berries

½ cup shredded coconut

1 cup granola

Chocolate syrup and whipped cream for garnish

DIRECTIONS

Peel the bananas, place on 4 plates, scoop the yogurt evenly on the bananas, and decorate the bananas with the rest of the ingredients. Garnish with the chocolate syrup and whipped cream.

158

CEREAL SHAKE
AKA TRAIL-MIX CEREAL

We all know that a correct diet and exercise is a good recipe for good health. But we need to put fun in that equation, too! Here you have a good breakfast mixed with exercise (shaking!), and I promise you: It's a fun way to start your day. There is really no right or wrong way to do this, so just have fun and be creative!

INGREDIENTS

Mixed dried fruit, such as raisins, dried cranberries, and dried cherries

Mix of cereals (whatever is in your cupboard)

Mixed nuts

Shredded coconut

Honey

DIRECTIONS

Fill a plastic cup with all your favorite ingredients. Close it with a slightly larger plastic cup (creating a shaker) and shake your mix! Eat it like that or add milk or yogurt.

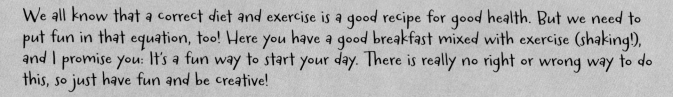

ACKNOWLEDGMENTS

There are many people I'd like to thank for helping me becoming Chef Gino. Of course, my family: Laura, Ada, and Rocco; Pina, Barbara, Andrea, and Flavio, who was instrumental in bringing me to the States to open a new chapter in my life. My aunt Anna, Graziano, Maura and Enrico, Irene, Simone, Sara, and Alessandro.

But then the list gets longer. Alessandro Bassi, who always believed in me and helped me keep going. Pilo, Roberto, Gianni, the childhood friends of so many adventures. Pappo, Rita, and Augusto, who always made me feel loved. I want to thank Alex for opening the door to a world beyond the little square I was born in.

I need to thank Luca Pelagatti for teaching me not to take everything so seriously and my schoolmates from 4E at Istituto Magistrale for always making me feel special.

I owe so much to my dear American friends: Ian, Gabriella, Pietro, Teresa, Sue, Portia, Jon, Carl, and their children, who I feel are like my children. Lilian and Tina and the dream we shared. And then Vinnie, Sara, Lori, Nicolas, and all my other friends both in Italy and in the States. Too many to mention—you know who you are.

A special shout-out to the Mar Vista Futball players: I'll see you tomorrow morning!

I also want to thank Eric for calling me up out of the blue one January morning and asking me to make a book: this one.

Maurizio, Zio Sergio, nonna Ada e nonno Ernesto, and my papa' Ettore, all smiling from above.

But I want to tell one more story.

In the introduction of the book, I talked about the owner of the local grocery store: Signora Rina. We would shop there all the time and sometimes we had the money to pay and sometimes we didn't. Signora Rina would then mark the amount we owned and add it to a list that would grow longer and longer. A list she ripped the day she retired. I ran into her years later, fresh from my success on Disney Channel in America. She was in a cafe in my old neighborhood with a relative. I hugged her as I would hug an aunt and told her about the States, about my adventures. I insisted to pay for cappuccino and brioche for her and her relative, but she wouldn't let me. I wanted to do something for her as small as that gesture was. She told me I owed her nothing and that her reward was seeing me doing so well in life. You don't see Chef Gino crying too often, but that morning I did. So finally I want to thank my lucky stars for having been born in that little square, in the poorest neighborhood in Parma.

Grazie!

163

INDEX

Underscored references indicate sidebars and tables. **Boldface** references indicate photographs.